Twilight Reflections

Where the Elderly Find God

By

Greg Hadley

Copyright 2011

MAY YOU ALWAYS FEEL GOD'S
PRESENCE IN YOUR LIFE.

Greg Hadley

DECEMBER 2011

Hadley, Greg (1934 -   )
Twilight Reflections / Greg Hadley—1st edition

ISBN-13   978-1-4679-3203-5
ISBN-10   1-4679-3203-5

Printed in the United States of America
First Edition

OTHER BOOKS BY GREG HADLEY

Fundamentals of Baseball Umpiring [1]

Common Problems; Common Sense Solutions [2]

100 Everyday Epiphanies:
    Simple Events That Can Inspire Prayer

God's Words to My Heart

Aging – The Autumn Phase of Life

[1] In the National Baseball Hall of Fame, Cooperstown, N. Y.

[2] Translated into Chinese for distribution and sale in the Asia-Pacific region.

TABLE OF CONTENTS

FOREWORD

Greg Hadley and I, together with our wives, have lived happily in Mary's Woods Retirement Community for several years. It occurs to me, however, that some of his personal identity labels and mine might seem opposite to some. He is a Roman Catholic with an outstanding career in business. I am a Protestant with a career as a pastor and teacher. Nonetheless, we clearly share some crossover spiritual callings. He has served his church as a volunteer teacher and hospital chaplain and also has sought out and written about spiritual practices and Protestant viewpoints. I earned a Doctor of Ministry degree in the field of Spiritual Direction from a Jesuit seminary and have taught this subject at a Benedictine seminary and a Jesuit university.

This two-person compatibility that Greg and I enjoy provides one small hint of the large value that a wide variety of readers is likely to discover in the one hundred vignettes of this fine book, which is in a genre similar to his previous one, *100 Everyday Epiphanies.* Greg not only keenly observes a vast array of real-life human situations and the responses he describes but also earnestly shares very illuminating personal experiences, attitudes, feelings, foibles, desires, prayers and awakenings of his own. My experience in prayerful reading of his pages has demonstrated to me that his personal openness facilitates my honest perception of both my own attitudes and the Lord's beckoning me to participate in His.

I believe that anyone who reads a page of the book and asks what personal intimations are implied is sure to receive benefit.

Greg has even provided to me in this book expansive hints that relate as well to three other sayings that I've chosen to live with. On a plaque beside my apartment door (from Erasmus, by way of Carl Jung): *"Bidden or not bidden, God is present."* From Marcus Aurelius: *"The soul is dyed the color of our inmost thoughts. "*From Jesus Christ (Matthew 24:42 et al.) *"Keep awake, therefore, for you do not know on what day your Lord is coming."*

May each person who reads and ponders this book be similarly carried into expanded awareness and life.

Rev. Forster W. Freeman
D. Min.

PREFACE

Except for the most reclusive among us, our daily lives are composed of serial encounters with people, places and things or events. Aside from a very few, most of these circumstances are quite routine, uneventful or inconsequential. We proceed throughout the day giving little thought to the neighbor we passed on the pathway, that flower we admired in our garden, the television news report we glanced at or the roadway we traveled to and from the market. Even the occurrence of something more significant only captures our attention for a short while unless we determine it directly affects us.

I believe most humans could describe their daily routine as looking into the eyepiece of a kaleidoscope—lots of random color and shapes but not much discernable form. I am not making a negative assessment here; I just don't think most folks give a lot of weight to the individual parts of their dawn-to-dusk existence. Neither do I believe we search for much meaning in our regular and often tedious activities. I think we are missing a real opportunity to get in touch with something important.

This book has a specific context. I am approaching eighty years old and I live in a continuing care retirement community named Mary's Woods located in Lake Oswego, Oregon. My age is important because I probably use a specific set of filters when observing, hearing or thinking about things happening in my life and the people I interact with. My neighbors in this community are, more or less, in the same circumstances as I am and we represent a growing subset of the larger community.

Yes, my neighbors are old, some of us are decrepit or facing declining health—but we seniors still have our minds and are able to offer important insights to what life is really about. We don't have all the answers but many of us have been thinking about the questions for a lot longer than our younger friends.

So, what is this missed opportunity I mentioned? I believe each of us can find meaning in the most mundane of human activities. It takes reflection plus a belief that I can peel back the layers of the simplest incident in my life and discover a kernel of significance...sometimes basic, sometimes profound...in every moment. Wisdom, insight and value can be plucked from each human encounter, observation or event that intersects with my life's vector. Is it important for me to discover insight with each new tick of the clock? Probably not. What if I missed some knowledge or understanding that was right in front of me? It's not the end of the world. But, here is the point: we should always be looking for these moments of understanding and clarity. Why? Because God does not come to us in lightning bolts or shouts from the rooftops. No, God is present to each of us in silent moments when we hear His voice speaking to us in whispers.

For all time, mankind has asked, "What is the meaning of life?" For those of us of faith, the simple answer to this question is found in the old Catholic Baltimore Catechism that states, "To know, love and serve God in this world and be happy with Him in the next." Who knows? By looking deeper into what is going on in my own anonymous life, I may find reinforcement for this basic Catechism text.

This little book contains one hundred stories about people, places and things I have experienced in my own life. Notice that many of these vignettes are simple ideas.

Each story is followed by a moral, an idea that seeks the significance of the story. It is a reflection of what I took away from the account as a small sliver of insight. Finally, each story concludes with a prayer seeking help from God in integrating the lesson into my persona.

This book is a sequel to one I wrote several years ago titled, "*100 Everyday Epiphanies – Simple Events in Life That Can Inspire Prayer.*" In that prior book, I noted that every reader could probably think of least one hundred incidents from their own lives that would be better than the ones I presented. I feel that way about this latest book, too. I urge you to look beyond the humdrum situations of your daily lives. Try to hear God's quiet voice instructing you about your own salvation story. With a little practice, I feel sure you will be enriched by what you hear and see and feel as life marches past.

I think this book is best read one page per day. Determine if the slice-of-life story resonates with you because of similar experiences in your own life. Next, I hope you see relevance in the moral, something that you have thought about, too. Finally, carefully read the prayer and see if it touches your spirit in any way. We're all different; I recognize that some of what I have written may not affect you one way or another. Neither of us needs to worry about that. If just one page in this entire book inspires you in a significant manner, then I will be pleased with the overall results of my efforts because I have helped you grasp some meaning by my writing.

Now a word about the title of this book. *Twilight* is that period near sunset when the day is coming to an end. While I still feel full of life, statistics indicate that I cannot expect to enjoy too many more years. Therefore, I consider this book as being written near the twilight of my life. *Reflection* means fixing ones thoughts on a concept or idea after careful consideration and meditation. Most of my stories come from this type of reflection. So, the title of this book, "Twilight Reflections," seemed very appropriate to me.

I am most appreciative for all the encouragement I received as I wrote this book. I especially thank Father Dick Berg CSC and my wife, Evie, for their constant support and to Rev. Forster Freeman for writing the Foreword.

I dedicate this work to my fourteen grandchildren, each of whom I love very much. I pray that God will protect them throughout their lives.

STAN

I sat with my dear friend Stan one sunny morning, in quiet conversation. His doctor had recently delivered ominous news—an aggressive stage-five cancer filled Stan's lungs.

"What are your thoughts?", I asked. "Do you feel apprehension or fear of what is coming?" I was gently trying to lead Stan into a discussion about death and what might lie beyond. He was not a churchgoer or religious. But he was a principled, decent man who lived out the Golden Rule in his daily interactions with others. "I've had a wonderful life," Stan declared. "The nine years since my retirement I considered a bonus, a blessing." With eyes slightly glistening from a hint of tears, he softly said, "I'll surely miss all of you but I know none of us get out of here alive. My time is up. If I find God on the other side, I'm sure He will know I did my best. So, I guess you could say I'm ready."

Acceptance. It is our assent to a situation that cannot be changed. When there are no more loopholes we finally quit struggling and let reality overtake us. Acceptance often brings us peace, calmness and serenity. Stan was a perfect model of that. Echoing his thoughts, I surely miss him.

God of cheerful acceptance,
I am confident that I'm always in charge of my life.
I know how to avoid any loss of control that I might face
I have carefully planned how to avoid all dead end roads.
Jesus says to me this is false logic.
He gently tells me His infinite will always prevails.
Our daily prayer is, "Thy will be done."
And so it is.

RIVER ROAD WALK

Near my home is a street named River Road. It is just a few steps from the Willamette River in Lake Oswego, Oregon. A walk along this road on a warm summer's day calms the soul. Trees line the path and the view across the river is lovely. Expansive homes on the opposite shore are inviting, their lawns are green and boat docks are well maintained. Occasionally a motorboat will pass by, briefly interrupting the quiet tranquility. I walk north and leave River Road, entering a beautiful forested area on a wide meandering path. The river stays in view most of the time as I finally reach George Rogers Park. Throughout my thirty-minute walk, I have seen God's creation exhibited to me in its awesome splendor.

Each of us needs refreshment and renewal once in awhile. The cares and worries of life beset us daily and the frenetic pace of events leaves us exhausted. This brief stroll permits each of my senses to be renewed. The sunlight filtered through the trees, the gentle lapping sounds of the river, fragrant grass and flowers, the touch of warm sunlight on my skin, the cold water I drink from the fountain—I feel like a new person.

God Who makes all things new,
I often take the wonders of creation for granted.
Daily opportunities to see You in nature are ignored.
Please, Lord, give me the grace to see beauty around me.
Don't let me be indifferent to the loveliness in the world.
You've placed the grandeur of Your handiwork before me.
Remind me of Your presence in all creation I see.

THE IMPERFECT GAME

A "perfect game" in baseball occurs when the pitcher retires all twenty-seven batters he faces with no one reaching base. It has happened only twenty times in professional baseball history. In 2010 a pitcher named Armando Gallaraga retired the first twenty-six batters he faced. The last batter hit a routine ground ball for what should have been the final out. A competent umpire, Jim Joyce, blew the call at first base, declaring the runner safe and ruining the perfect game. Instead of exploding in anger, the pitcher shrugged his shoulders and accepted the obvious mistake. He returned to the mound and retired the next batter. After the game, Joyce saw a replay on TV and was mortified by his error. Contrary to the accepted "code of conduct" he rushed to the players' locker room to apologize to Gallaraga. To the press, the pitcher said, "Nobody's perfect. Jim's a good umpire. He just made a mistake on that one call."

Could I have been so forgiving when such a huge injustice had been done to me? In a game where umpires never say "I'm sorry", could I have been like Joyce and immediately sought the forgiveness of the one I've harmed? I wonder.

God of perfect forgiveness,
I am often offended by things said to me or done to me.
I seethe and look for ways to obtain revenge.
Why is my spirit so full of corrosive acid?
The young pitcher is a wonderful example of forgiveness.
The umpire shows me how and when to seek pardon.
Why don't these simple acts of humanity come easily to me?
As usual, Lord, I need Your grace to change my heart.

THE HOMELESS MAN

A company I managed required a twenty-mile one-way commute across the streets of Los Angeles. It was a dreadful daily grind. Along the way, I noticed a middle aged man walking. He was disheveled, dirty and appeared mentally ill. Day after day I saw him; could I help? Did he need money? Clothes? Where did he live? Would I be safe approaching him? I assembled a bag of clothes, soap, toiletries and basic food and loaded it into my car. I didn't see my "friend" for a couple of days. Was he sick—or dead? Finally, I spotted him and pulled to the curb. My heart was pounding; I could not anticipate his reaction. He approached me and I held out the bag to him. In apparent panic, he fled down the street and ducked into an alley. I followed, scared at what I might encounter. Not finding him, I left the bag at the head of the alley hoping he would eventually find it and use the contents.

Sometimes help is easy to give. Other times, it can be complicated. It is rewarding to be the giver. The person receiving help often finds it difficult or awkward. Throughout our lives, we must sometimes give and sometimes receive.

God of gracious assistance and aid to all,
I often miss obvious opportunities to help others.
Is that because some people shield their need of help?
Perhaps I avert my gaze to avoid "getting involved."
There seem to be endless situations where I could assist.
So many, in fact, that I would be drained of time and money.
I know I can't solve the whole world's needs.
But help me to kindly support those who are nearest to me.

THE BEEKEEPER

A neighbor is a beekeeper. He keeps two boxes of hives at our retirement community. Recently, he was invited to speak about this hobby to the residents. He made a fascinating explanation of the highly organized social model the bees use to get all the necessary work done in the hives, to protect their queen and themselves and to produce honey. The Queen is at the top of the hive hierarchy, producing as many as 2,000 eggs per day, in season. Some of the larvae mature producing worker bees that pollinate flowers and plants to make honey. Drones, described as "useless males," have one job—to fertilize the Queen. Worker bees do some basic cleaning and hive-tending chores for approximately the first twenty-one days of their lives. Then they go out to do the crucial work of pollinating and to gather honey. After about forty-five days of life, their usefulness over, the worker bees die.

Human lives often pass by quickly, too. For most, growing up years are followed by productive adulthood, aging and eventual death. Bees play a vital role on our planet as do we humans. Our gifts may be simple but each of us can achieve great things leaving a legacy for our loved ones.

God of all life,
I am allotted a certain time on earth.
I can use these minutes and months as I wish.
Will it be for good or ill?
That is up to me.
The wise will spend their lives in things that glorify You.
Help me to always build up Your kingdom on earth.
When death comes, let me be counted as fruitful.

THE AMAZING HUMAN SPIRIT

Who could forget the story of the Chilean miners entombed deep in the earth? The astounding rescue of these men touched hearts throughout the world. Eventual success was credited to special drilling equipment, creative engineers, behavioral experts and the improvisational skills of the rescuers on site. Prayer should be included. Personal bravery was routinely observed. The event was a testament to the human spirit. Facing death, these men maintained cheerful and hopeful attitudes. Even in their bleak situation, a hierarchy of leadership was established, daily chores assigned and all worked together to support the group. Everyone pitched in to manage food, dispense medicines, handle sanitation, create historical journals and share spiritual comfort and humor. Where did this determination, patience, hope and resiliency come from? Finally, what kind of courage was required to enter the rescue capsule to ascend 2,000 feet through a black, claustrophobic tunnel? Truly, this was a remarkable example of humanity dealing with death, entombment and final resurrection.

Even a small matter can cause us to become discouraged, distraught or hopeless. Feeling sorry for yourself? Think what the Chilean miners endured. Most of the difficulties we face pale next to their situation.

God of all hope,
I often feel broken and battered by life's trials.
My situation seems desperate and hopeless.
Like Job, I cry out, "I have no rest, for trouble comes."
Why do I not see that God is with me always?

LAND OF THE RISING SUN

A massive earthquake, followed by a devastating tsunami and the subsequent mortal danger from damaged nuclear facilities: how many crushing blows must be delivered to bring a nation to its knees? Even the highly organized social fabric of the Japanese people could not withstand nature's incredible force. In spite of this disaster, we heard of many unselfish acts of neighborly concern; sharing food, water, shelter and supplies without considering repayment or reciprocity. Would we in this country be as generous and caring under similar circumstances? Perhaps. Just when you think society is in the grip of a don't-give-a-damn attitude, we marvel at how neighbors care for one another after tornadoes, floods and similar violent natural disasters. These life-altering events sometimes evoke reprehensible actions like looting, price gouging and hoarding but most often we see the kinder, gentler and more loving side of human nature. The devastating spring storms and flooding of 2011 in the southeast United States provided a perfect example of love-your-neighbor in action. Hope is still alive.

Why does it often require a catastrophe to reveal the loving, caring part of our nature? Wouldn't it be wonderful if all of us were loving, caring neighbors everyday of our lives?

God of gracious love,
Help me find Your face in the face of my neighbor.
Remind me that I claim to love You, Who is unseen, but often fail to love my neighbor whom I do see. Teach me that I should love others always, not just when trouble strikes.

THE SYMPHONY ORCHESTRA

We often attend performances of the Oregon Symphony Orchestra. Arriving several minutes before the concert starts, we observe the musicians taking their places on stage and warming up their instruments. Violins, violas, basses, cellos, tubas, French horns, flutes, trombones, trumpets and all the rest create a discordant and unpleasant cacophony lasting several minutes as each member readies his or her instrument for today's selection of music. Finally, an anticipatory hush falls over the hall. An oboe—because of its consistent tuning--plays an "A" note and the instruments are given a final adjustment under the direction of the concert master. All is now in readiness. The conductor mounts the podium, raises the baton and the orchestra begins. Shrill dissonance a few moments before becomes beautiful, disciplined even rhapsodic music. The audience is lifted up by lilting harmony and the welcome wave of sound flowing from all the instruments.

There are similar examples in our daily life. Voices in our public square often shout discordant and conflicting ideas about how things should be. No one listens to anyone else. Debate devolves into strident screaming. How do we bring harmony out of this chaos? Can our public debate become moderated, at the very least?

God of all sweet harmony,
I must learn to hear my neighbor.
He has a viewpoint that I must listen to.
Yes, he may be wrong, but he deserves my attention.
Maybe I am wrong, and I want him to listen to me, too.
We both need Your help to bring harmony to our lives.

CHAIR YOGA CLASSES

Two or three times a week, I attend a chair yoga class. My medical doctor told me that the deep breathing featured in yoga and the low impact stretching would probably be better for me than weight training in the gym. A typical class has about twenty participants including three or four men. The forty-five minute sessions contain lots of exercises to stretch the spine, ankles, shoulders, arms, legs and hands—all done as we practice deep breathing techniques. Everything is accomplished while we are seated. The program is more strenuous than you might think. The room is darkened and there is soft music playing in the background as we go through the poses. We are encouraged to keep our eyes closed so we don't become concerned about how we are performing relative to others. That's a good idea because the ability and flexibility present in our group varies considerably. I leave these sessions quite energized, but also very relaxed.

Most of us experience so much tension in our daily lives. Wouldn't it be wonderful if we could incorporate habitual techniques to keep us relaxed in the face of daily anxiety?

God of peace and tranquility,
Tension and stress seem to surround me like a bubble.
Be careful, don't fall.
Did I take my medications this morning?
How will I make my medical appointment this afternoon?
I cannot find that important paperwork my bank requires.
Worry about my grandchild fills my days and nights.
Lord, help me to relax.
Let me turn things over to You.
You can deal with these things much better than I can.

THE CENTENARIAN'S iPAD

Most of us old-timers decry our lack of competence about computers, cell phones and all the latest electronic gadgets. Grandchildren try to teach us how these things work but often with little success. We either don't grasp the basic concepts or can't remember which control buttons to push from one hour to the next. I should not paint all of us seniors with the same brush. Living in our retirement community is a bright, energetic, smart and articulate woman named Virginia who was recently introduced to the Apple iPad by her children. She immediately embraced this new device and began using it to perform many tasks previously difficult for her to accomplish. She arranged demonstrations for all her neighbors, enthusiastically pointing out how they could benefit from such a device as well. She even contacted Apple executives offering to be a senior citizen spokesperson promoting this new product; they were intrigued. By the way, did I mention that Virginia is almost 101 years old?

The process of aging is poorly measured by the number of years one has lived. All of us have the capacity to grow in wisdom, knowledge and the love of life no matter our age.

God of youth and the elderly,
To the young, time seems dreamily suspended.
Horizons are infinitely distant, hazy destinations.
The old see more clearly the rapid passing of earthly life.
But, as the clock ticks down toward midnight, there is still time to learn, to love, to grow.
Help me to use every moment of my life to honor You.

THE HOSPITAL CHAPLAIN

I am a volunteer chaplain at a local general hospital. Legacy Meridian Park is licensed for 150 beds and has many nearby offices for the doctors who practice in the facility. The hospital is well regarded in the community and has gained recognition for excellence in several areas of patient care. Excluding the doctors, there are about 900 people who staff the hospital. They provide nursing, security, housekeeping, maintenance, administration, food and other services required to sustain smooth operations. Of the total staff, over 300 are volunteers. You will see these people in their distinctive light blue jackets throughout the facility managing the gift stores, providing escort services for patients, assisting nurses on the wards, being chaplains, greeters and in many other activities. Yearly hours worked by volunteers would cost the hospital millions of dollars if completed by paid staff, states the Administrator.

This is just one of countless examples of people giving their time in service to others. Volunteers remind us of our call to exercise basic goodness in life. On final judgment day, I believe we will be partially measured based on selfless time we invest in the well being of our brothers and sisters.

God of all compassion for others,
My daily life is hectic and over-filled with activity.
Time is often considered the most precious of commodities.
I never seem to have enough for myself or my loved ones.
Lord, teach me how to carve out a little time for my neighbors.
While I extend a helping hand to others, to strangers, I may very well meet You face to face.
(Matt. 25: 40)

11

THE MUSICIANS

I have two neighbors who were world-class musicians during the prime of their lives. Annette was so talented that she played the piano in Carnegie Hall, New York City. Even now, well into her eighties, she will occasionally perform for the residents of our retirement center on a Sunday afternoon. Annette still possesses a lilting yet powerful style on the grand piano. Jim gained his fame as a church organist and choir director. He garnered many awards and commendations for the brilliance of his work. Even though Jim stayed with one church for many years, he was in great demand around the world as a guest artist or teacher. He loves to play the piano for his friends after dinner in our social lounge. Annette and Jim have the sweetest, most engaging personalities you could ever hope to encounter. Both of these lovely people have been forced to deal with some cognitive impairment in their latter years. It is difficult to see talented people struggling to maintain their skills while a diminished human body fiercely imposes limits on their abilities.

How will I deal with life when age or disease erodes my former capabilities? These two people have shown me courageous examples of how God's gifts should be used to benefit all.

God of the elderly and infirm,
Over my lifetime You loaned me many talents and skills.
You nudged me to use these gifts to build up Your kingdom.
As I age, I find You are recalling these abilities from me.
Do You plan to now share them with others more capable?
If so, let them know I tried to use them for Your benefit.

THE GALAXY OF TECHNOLOGY

Have you ever been up at the darkest part of night, walking through the main living area of your residence? Wherever you look you will see small lights. The television, stereo disk player, portable telephone cradles, microwaves, and clocks—all announce their low power use to me. I also see blinking lights on ceiling smoke detectors and fire alarms. The four green lights of my computer's modem tell me it's ready to go. All these lights remind me how technology has intruded into my life. Fifty years ago, the only electrical gadgets in my home were a radio and toaster. Little by little, I began to acquire those can't-live-without-them devices. Now, they are everywhere, a constant reminder of how dependent I have become on this equipment for my entertainment, information, safety and interaction with others. A summer storm or a fallen tree that disrupts my electrical service can leave me without light, heat, television, air conditioning and even a phone.

Think of those in the community that rely on electricity to operate their respirators, dialysis machines or other medical devices. My selfish whining about "missing my favorite TV program" shows how thoughtless I have become for others who truly depend on electrical power for their lives.

God, Creator of all things,
I have become a certified member of the consumer society.
I expect, no, demand, a constant source of reliable electricity.
Our power grid is dependable; I will accept no less.
What of other communities in the world?
Is there acceptable power in Honduras? Pakistan? Iraq?
I doubt it. Why do I always require a preferential option?

THE NUNS' GRAVEYARD

The principal building in our retirement community is a former convent for Catholic nuns. Now totally refurbished, this beautiful old building still provides a retirement home for about forty nuns. Nearby the previous convent is a lovely, serene graveyard containing the remains of many sisters, as well as a few priests who served as chaplains over the years. The cemetery is wonderfully maintained and is surrounded by large trees that take on dramatic fall hues when autumn arrives. A walk through the graveyard represents a mini-history lesson. Located on the corner of the property, this quiet, peaceful place allows me to get in touch with these holy women who went before me and did so much to build God's kingdom here on earth. I wonder about their personalities and foibles when they lived and what eternal life must mean to them now. This also makes me think about that time—not too far away—when I shall be at rest someplace. Wherever that may be, I hope it is as tranquil and invitingly quiet as this site feels to me. Who will come to visit my grave, I wonder?

I hear on each Ash Wednesday, "Remember, you are dust and to dust you will return." How can I best deal with this reality? I think I am called to live each day as if it were my last.

God, source of eternal life,
It is difficult to visualize my own personal end of life.
Each new day finds me one day older.
But, I still have plans and see things on distant horizons.
Someday I must experience my final moment on this earth.
I know this is true, but I still cannot envision it clearly.
Help me to be ready, Lord, when my allotted time is complete.

PARAPROSDOKIANS

A *paraprosdokian* is a figure of speech in which the latter part of a sentence or phrase is surprising or unexpected in a way that causes the reader to reframe or reinterpret the first part. It is frequently used for humorous or dramatic effect, sometimes producing an anticlimax. Following are a few examples of paraprosdokians:

- Going to church doesn't make you a Christian any more than standing in a garage makes you an automobile.
- We never really grow up; we only learn to act in public.
- Dolphins are so smart that within a few weeks of being captured they can train people to stand on the edge of the pool and throw them fish.
- "I didn't say it was your fault. I said I was blaming you."
- You don't need a parachute to skydive. You only need a parachute to skydive twice.
- I know the voices I hear in my head are not real but they do have some really good ideas.
- When tempted to fight fire with fire, remember that the fire department usually uses water.
- You're never too old to learn, or do, something stupid.

Yes, these are amusing sayings. But, there is a kernel of truth and wisdom in most of them, too. I should probably pay more attention instead of dismissing these things after a good laugh.

God of all joy and mirth,
Please keep me well supplied with rib-tickling humor.
Show me that a good joke often contains some wisdom too.
I frequently take life too seriously.
Help me to look past the gravity and enjoy the fun.

BART

Bart had led a difficult life. His youth was dominated by drugs, alcohol and crime. While committing a robbery one night he was shot by a police officer. The bullet ripped through Bart's spine leaving him a paraplegic. In his late thirties, Bart found God. He joined a group of people seeking admission to the Catholic Church. He faithfully attended all the sessions and I could see the Holy Spirit working in him. Prior to his baptism at Easter, Bart asked to address the congregation at Mass one Sunday morning. With tremendous courage and grace, Bart told about his previous life and how thrilled he was that he would soon become a Catholic. His riveting talk was delivered to a hushed church; I observed many crying. Concluding his presentation, Bart introduced the police officer who had shot him. Over time, they had become close friends. The policeman had greatly influenced Bart in seeking a new life of productivity and love of God. These two men, one in a wheel chair, the other standing, presented a memorable example of reconciliation and brotherly love.

It's easy for me to give up on someone. They are out of control and their behavior is unacceptable. God says, "I love you unconditionally just the way you are." Can't I do the same?

God, source of all filial love,
You must teach me how to give unconditional love.
My standards of behavior for others are rigid and inviolate.
When I see people failing to live up to my code of conduct,
I quickly write them off; nothing can save them, I think.
You are quick to give them a hand to lift them up.
Please show me how to treat them just as You do.

THE SISTER SISTERS

Among my neighbors are several Holy Names nuns who have sibling sisters living in the community as well. I refer to these pairs as the "sister Sisters." Some share apartments. It is interesting to see how these sisters interact and get along now as elderly religious women. Of course, I expect to see an obvious outpouring of love and care from those who have spent their lives providing attentive care to others. But, I am also sure there must be little aggravations that crop up between most family members. Occasional annoyances can hardly be avoided. That's true for all of us, not just sisters who happen to be nuns. I have witnessed great human love shown by these sisters to one another; if there are any spats or arguments, they are well hidden. What a wonderful example of Christian love for each other!

We are each called to "love our neighbor as ourselves." Easy to say, but often difficult to do. I deeply loved my sister and brother. That was in spite of the many ways we personally aggravated one another. I have other brothers and sisters in the Body of Christ that I do not love as I should. Who gave me permission to pick and choose whom I would love?

Savior God, a member of the Holy Family,
The "sister Sisters" practice filial love at its best.
They cherish siblings, even those who exhibit foibles.
I experienced the same things with my own family.
What of those people I encounter in the Body of Christ?
Can I be selective about which of them I will love?
"No," says Jesus, "you're all in this together."
Lord, I cannot love all people without Your Grace and help.

THE SOUP KITCHEN

There is a soup kitchen downtown serving the homeless. My wife and I have volunteered there; it is quite an experience and different than I expected. The volunteers begin by having dinner—the same food we will dispense later. The soup was tasteless and thin and the bread was not fresh. That was a pointed reminder of how different our lives are from those we will serve. We began to work in cramped quarters packed with those awaiting a meal. I expected to see grateful eyes and thankful smiles from folks happy to have some solid food, a cup of hot coffee and a chance to come in out of the cold, wet evening. Instead, I saw sullen faces, eyes that would not contact mine, and impatience for faster service and a larger portion than I had already served. Most people looked dirty and smelled worse. What had I gotten myself into?

Why should I expect lavish thanks for mediocre food, praise for my service or joy for a few minutes inside? These people live brutal lives ravaged by addictions, mental illness, poverty, and abandonment by family, or simple bad luck. I was ashamed of my attitude, acting like some liege lord tossing scraps from my table to the local peasants. This is not who I am called to be. Jesus wants us to be foot-washing people. I think that means giving care for the most needful among us.

God of all gracious hospitality,
I would prefer not to associate with dirty, homeless people.
They offend my sensibilities about the way one should act.
But where can I expect to truly see the face of God?
If I look hard enough, it will be found in a soup kitchen line.
Help me to seek You there, Lord; it isn't easy to do so.

FASCINATION WITH CELEBRITY

If I took a poll of TV programs being watched by my neighbors, the celebrity shows like "American Idol" and "Dancing with the Stars" would surely rank very high. These productions offer harmless, "feel good" entertainment, but why are we seemingly obsessed with the celebrities who perform on them? Perhaps we fantasize that when we were younger, more alluring, better athletes or singers, that we could have appeared on these shows, too. Now, we are enthralled with these young, energetic and attractive personalities and think: "They will really go far in this world." Well, maybe that's true. But have you noticed that most of the great achievements in life are accomplished by average, obscure women and men? Great teachers, doctors and nurses, scientists, engineers, Moms and Dads and public servants are rarely recognized for the excellence in their lives. Millions of daily acts of kindness and love go unrecognized by the general public. I doubt we will ever see a television show titled, *"Average People Doing Their Best to Help a Neighbor."*

It is OK for me to strive for my personal "fifteen minutes of fame." I am also sure it is better for me to use my unique talents and skills to strive for excellence in my vocation, be the best neighbor I can be and make a positive contribution to society. I'll try to be an "American Idol" to one person today.

God Who encourages us all to do our best,
It's human nature to want recognition for my achievements.
I enjoy basking in the limelight or hear, "You did great!"
Is God going to check me for medals and awards?
When I meet Him face to face, what will He ask me?
"Did you love? Were you a friend? Did you do your best?"

TRYON CREEK PARK

Portland, Oregon, has many "urban forests." These unique and beautiful places allow me to quickly leave the city's frenetic pace and step into a tranquil and peaceful environment. Tryon Creek Park is nearby. Its northern boundary is a busy, well-traveled street. I can park my car on the side of this road, and fifty paces into the park, I am surrounded by lovely old Douglas firs, alders and spruce trees. Navigating the rugged natural paths, I am completely insulated from street noise within a minute of entering the area. I can spend hours in this forest, observing the delicate wild flowers, hiking the trails beside trickling streams and losing myself in my own reveries. While the park has many visitors, I will seldom encounter others during my stay. When I finally work my way back to the car, I feel deliciously refreshed and rejuvenated. The cares, tensions and worries of life have evaporated under the dappled light shining through the giant trees.

Some of us dread solitude and silence. Why? We all need an urban forest to visit each day, whether it is actual or virtual. Quiet time without the intrusion of radio, iPod music or other electronic distraction is essential for my mental and spiritual health. Sometimes listening, even listening to the sounds of silence, is the best therapy any of us can have. Try it.

God of all natural beauty,
Living in an urban setting leaves me feeling claustrophobic.
I am hemmed in by people, buildings, activities and noise.
I crave solitude, silence, a chance to think and pray.
I can retreat to my urban forest; others will seek a quiet nook.
Help us all, Lord, to set a daily time to be alone with You.

AN INVITATION TO THE VATICAN

In December 2010, there was a Pontifical Conference on "Aging and the Coming Health Care Crisis" at the Vatican. Because I had written a book about the practical aspects of aging, I was invited to be a presenter at this event. Feelings of excitement, inadequacy and humbleness flooded me when I was asked to participate. The other speakers were prominent, world-class experts on various aspects of the subject. I had merely written a simple little book about life in a retirement community. "Why me?", I thought. "I have neither status nor expertise to join these other participants." I seriously considered declining the invitation. Then my friend, Father Dick Berg, CSC, set me straight. "This chance to share the ideas in your book is not just extended to you," Father Dick said. "It really relates to all your friends and neighbors that you wrote about. You will be representing them, not yourself." This sage advice provided the courage and acceptance I needed. I went to the Vatican and the entire experience was thrilling for me. My neighbors shared in my joy.

Pride and ego can be deadly vices. Genuine participation in community is always about others, not me. Like St. Paul, it is good to be knocked off my high horse now and again.

God our great teacher of humility,
It is obvious to me when I am given awards and honors.
After all, I possess several unique talents and skills.
But, all too often I forget those gifts are not mine.
They are merely on loan to me from God.
 "You must humbly use these blessings for the good of others.
I can take them away as easily as I gave them," says God.

EVIE'S SIXTEITH BIRTHDAY

I was eager to give my wife a memorable party on this milestone birthday. I created an elaborate ruse with the help of some business colleagues that there was to be an important meeting in Palm Springs over her birthday weekend. We could combine my business with our pleasure of visiting old friends in Southern California we hadn't seen for some time. Of course, the business meeting was fiction, but Evie didn't know that and agreed to go along. Meanwhile, our daughter, Leigh Anne, was contacting family and friends about coming to Palm Springs for a birthday weekend surprise party. The deception worked perfectly! To begin, our children were hiding in our hotel room when we checked in. New people showed up each day to join the fun. Evie was overwhelmed with love and friendship from all who came to celebrate with her. She recently told me that her memory isn't what it once was, but she remembers virtually every detail of that magical weekend party. We are reminded that great happiness is almost always a shared experience, not a solitary event.

I think giving happiness is even more enjoyable than receiving happiness. Sometimes my selfish nature causes me to forget this, but the simple act of giving joy is always rewarding.

God, source of all happiness,
Give me what I want; I'm sure that will make me happy.
Don't hold back, Lord; total pleasure is my personal goal.
You say it is better to give joy rather than to receive it?
I am unconvinced until I experience this for myself.
When I am able to cause pure happiness in others,
I find my spirit soaring. Thanks for reminding me, Lord.

JIGSAW PUZZLES

I don't much like board games. However, jigsaw puzzles, and the people who work them, do fascinate me. When I see all the small cutout shapes scrambled on a tabletop, it looks like so much chaos to me. Working with exquisite patience while using a simple picture to guide them, I watch others doggedly search for the next piece to add. Slowly the little pieces are attached one by one as the picture begins to take shape. From so many pieces how can these people possibly find the next piece that fits perfectly? I spent my business career dealing with complex problems, but seem not to be hard-wired for this activity. While many find jigsaws to be relaxing, entertaining and challenging, they drive me crazy and leave me breathless with frustration. Worst of all, after the triumph of successful completion the builder nonchalantly knocks down the work and boxes it all for another to tackle. This all goes against my grain: chaos, infinite patience, final triumph, and casual discard. It's like building an elaborate sand castle on the water's edge only to watch the evening tide wash it all away.

What can we learn from jigsaws? Dealing with complex events, circumstances and diverse people affects all our lives. With patience and persistence, we can form a beautiful mosaic from these things and people we encounter. While often frustrating, the end result can be most satisfying.

God Who makes order out of chaos,
My life seems complicated, full of people and moving parts.
Lacking patience, I often make a botch of relationships.
I know I could do a better job of dealing with life's events.
Help me, Lord, to form a lovely mosaic from my circumstances.

23

PEACE

Peace is something we all seek in life. In the Gospel of John, Chapter 14 we find these words Jesus spoke to his disciples: "Peace I leave with you; My peace I give to you. Do not let your hearts be troubled or afraid." Events seem to conspire against peace in my life. Health concerns, economic struggles, security and good choices for my children and grandchildren, global wars, environmental worries—these things leave me without peace and a heart that is anxious and afraid. Perhaps the greatest obstacle to peace is my constant need to be in control of life's events. I seem determined that my needs, goals and objectives are fulfilled exactly as I want them. To turn over these things to God with total trust is very risky business. What if things don't work out as I planned? Anxiety and worry will then surely override the peace I so desire. At some point in our lives most of us learn that we're *not* in control; rather it is God or some supreme spirit. I believe that only when this reality sinks in can I experience real peace.

As St. Claude de la Colombiere said, "One of the greatest gifts that the Holy Spirit can bestow on us is peace in time of struggle, calm in the midst of trouble, so that in time of desolation we are armed with a strong courage." Amen. *"Living with Christ"* May 2011 Edition, New London, CT. USA

God, the source of all peace,
I join others in dealing with the frantic pace of daily life.
So many things to do, places to be and lists to complete.
Calmness and peace are will-o-the-wisps, seldom enjoyed.
"I will help if you but let Me," the Holy Spirit whispers.
But, I think it is only my personal efforts that will work.
Lord, please show me how to trust You with my life.

SAFE DRIVING CLASSES

For several years, I taught a safe driving course to senior citizens. It was a worthwhile activity for the students and for me, too. We can't deny that advancing age makes it both risky and difficult to drive safely. We don't see or hear as well, our reflexes are slowing down and our strength, flexibility and agility are waning. The classes provided the students with techniques to compensate for their diminished abilities. A key part of the class focused on discerning when to stop driving. I could feel the tension in the room when I taught this segment. Many were eager, even desperate, to continue driving. Most felt that not driving would impact their life style negatively. In reality, the question is "when," not "if," we will stop driving. Having an alternative transportation plan is crucial when you make the transition to being a non-driver.

Life in general also requires a "Plan B." Many routine activities become difficult as we age. Climbing steps, hearing basic conversation, finding that certain foods no longer agree with us—there are many accommodations I must make in my senior years. Fighting the inevitable leads to bitter unhappiness. Accepting changes with a smile can offer a comfortable, cheerful existence lived a different way. Which is the better choice for you, do you think?

God the protector of all,
I still drive but avoid freeways and driving at night.
It never occurred to me that someday I wouldn't drive.
Now that time is visible to me on a nearby horizon.
Help me, Lord, to cheerfully accept this loss of privilege.
St. Philip Neri said, "A joyful heart is easily made perfect."

GENEROUS GIVING, RELUCTANT RECEIVING

I am not an anthropologist or social scientist but I know a problem with the human condition when I see one. And do we ever have a problem! Consider the situation of older people living in a close-knit community. Simply put, many people are willing and able to provide assistance to their neighbors by doing small errands, driving to medical appointments or picking up items while doing their own shopping. On the other hand, people who no longer drive or find it difficult to get around are extremely reluctant to ask for help or "bother" their neighbors for assistance. The generous "givers" are sincerely willing to help; the shy "takers" hate to think of asking for aid. There is an invisible wall between the two groups and no amount of discussion seems to break down this barrier. Is false pride the issue? By *asking* for assistance do I expose my weakness and vulnerability? Do I sound like I'm no longer capable of taking care of myself? When *offering* to do small tasks, do I sound superior or condescending? Is my generous offer really seen as an unenthusiastic social nicety? Can you identify with either one—or both—of these groups of people?

Community, by definition, involves shared experiences, interaction with people, give and take, and feelings for others. How am I called to play my part in making my community work?

God, Who calls us to care for our neighbor,
When strong and vibrant, I seek to help a neighbor and friend.
When weak and infirm, I need aid from a neighbor and friend.
How can I show my generous spirit in a loving way?
How can I show my grateful heart for generosity shown to me?
Either way, remind me of Your command: Love one another.

THE WOOD SHOP

Leo was one of my dearest friends. When he moved to our retirement community, he donated all the equipment from his extensive, state-of-the-art wood shop to the community's modest facility. Our sleepy little hobby shop suddenly became a beehive of woodworking activity, a true "sawdust factory," as they say. The new equipment permitted big, expansive jobs so lots of projects were launched. I know virtually nothing about working with wood but through Leo's encouragement I took on the job of building a wine storage cabinet. The trials and tribulations of that project are fodder for another book. Let me just say I got the job done—finally—with a lot of help and the finished product actually looked pretty good. I find it most interesting how one person can be a catalyst for such dramatic change. Leo's simple, generous act transformed not only the facility, but also the enthusiasm level of our woodworking residents. Basic raw lumber turned into beautiful pieces of furniture, shelving, bowls, and yes, wine bars. Truly, one person can make a real difference. What have I done lately to rekindle enthusiasm for life in people I interact with daily?

Don't spend your time looking for heroes. Forget about somebody else doing the right thing. Just remember life's ten most important little words: *If it is to be, it is up to me.*

God, the source of all our inspiration,
Leo, a humble man, made a choice to share with others.
He could not have anticipated how much good this would do.
His generosity inspired a new sense of enthusiasm for many.
Help me, Lord, to look for ways to lift up my neighbors.
Let me bear fruit thirty or sixty or a hundredfold. (Matt. 13)

MEMORIAL DAY

The last Monday of May. The start of summer activities. A three-day weekend providing a long break for many working people. Initially called Decoration Day, the graves of Civil War soldiers were marked with flowers and flags. More wars led to more graves; now we honor all those who have died for their country. Originally this was a solemn yearly commemoration of services at national cemeteries and somber speeches by dignitaries at public venues. Memorial Day has devolved into a day off work to take the family to the beach, on a picnic or to have a barbecue with friends or neighbors. The original meaning of this day is obscured by a perceived national craving for recreation and leisure. Do many even think about the silent sentinels who fill our national cemeteries? Sadly, we often have other priorities on Memorial Day. Our freedoms just "happened," didn't they? I have trouble identifying with those men and women who died to allow me to worship in the church of my choice, speak my mind, work and live where it is convenient and to elect my leaders with a secret ballot. How have we lost our sense of deep appreciation for our fallen?

"Men and women" die in battle? Many of them were just fuzzy- cheeked teenagers. They lost two lives: the one they were living and another that they never got a chance to live. We *must* remember their sacrifices for us.

God, Who loves both the living and the dead,
So many have died protecting my rights and freedoms.
Do I have appropriate appreciation for their great sacrifices?
Though sometimes justified, war creates terrible hardships.
Never let me forget those who have paid with their lives for me.

BINGO ON SUNDAY AFTERNOON

Twice a month my wife, Evie, conducts a Bingo game for residents where we live. There is an enthusiastic group of about fifteen people who show up on schedule. It costs $.10 per card per game and all the money is distributed to the winners. To me, it is a mindless and boring game, but don't tell that to the die-hard players. They think Bingo is a great diversion and a wonderful way to spend two hours on a Sunday afternoon. Frankly, Evie doesn't really like the game all that much, but she feels her effort brings a little cheer to a group who may not have much excitement in their lives.

My Catholic faith tells me I must be mindful of the *Corporal Works of Mercy*. To heed Christ's call to care for my neighbors I was taught I must feed the hungry; clothe the naked; give drink to the thirsty; house the homeless; visit the sick; visit the imprisoned and bury the dead. It doesn't say "run a Bingo game on Sunday afternoon to enliven someone's life." But I think of Evie's stint every other Sunday is a Corporal Work of Mercy to those who get so much enjoyment from the game. What can I do to bring happiness, entertainment and a little fun to others? For whatever that is, I am called to do so.

God, Who cares for the lowly and humble,
There are so many homeless, hungry and hurting people.
I cannot get to all of them but I help where I am able.
Distress is not always manifested just on "skid row."
Some pain is invisible: loneliness, sadness, depression.
Many well-fed, smartly dressed people also require my aid.
Lead me, Lord, to the places I am most needed.
I expect to be surprised at some of the locations.

NO GOOD DEED GOES UNPUNISHED

Our parish in Brea, California had a social outreach program called ACT - Active Christians Today. We were organized to provide temporary housing, food, clothing, furniture and other household items to destitute families in our area. One of our first clients was a family of five living in a station wagon. When we discovered them, we located an apartment, got utilities connected, stocked the kitchen with food, gave them some basic furniture and other things to set up a household. My crew delivered the last of the items including a television set. As I climbed the steps lugging the TV, I felt good about what we had done for this down-and-out family. "Where would you like the TV," I asked? When the TV was operating, the guy said to me, "Is this the best you can do—a lousy black and white TV? My kids are used to color." The nerve of this guy! I wanted to punch him in the nose!

After calming down, I distinctly saw the Holy Spirit at work. Those of us who had so self-righteously done our Christian duty wanted nothing but fawning praise and gratitude from the recipients of our assistance. "See-look at how good we are. You're wretched and unworthy of our help; but we are so good and we gave you this aid, even though you don't deserve it." Jesus said, "I have come to serve, not to be served." What a wake-up call and lesson this encounter turned out to be.

God, servant of the servants,
What is the source of my haughtiness of spirit?
Look at the true givers: Teresa of Calcutta, John XXIII.
They clearly understood their role in modeling You.
Help me, Lord, to see Your face in everyone I try to help.

CATASTROPHES – MAN MADE

Recently there have been many disasters caused by the collapse of man-made systems, technology or simple human failure. The levies around New Orleans ruptured during Hurricane Katrina; an Air France jet from South America dropped into the sea; a massive oil spill in the Gulf of Mexico caused death and economic peril; an interstate bridge collapsed in Minnesota. This is a short list of many calamities that have befallen us. These were not Acts of God. In every instance, a piece of technology, a man-made system or a human being caused these events. What is a typical reaction to these situations? Fingers are pointed: Who's to blame? Who can be sued? This is followed by hand wringing about what can be done to prevent this from ever happening again. The cycle is repeated endlessly. But, we are not gods that create foolproof computers, machines or systems. To accept this truth requires us to admit we are human, and therefore, fallible. This concept is a horror to some.

This provides an important life lesson. We attempt to be helpful and compassionate to our neighbor, living the Golden Rule each day. But we often fail. Failure is not forever. We must pick ourselves up and try again. That is the essence of what it means to be human.

God of all perfection,
I am often my own harshest critic, especially when I fail.
"I have made that same stupid mistake again," I cry.
Lord, show me how to get up and try to do better next time.
Jesus fell on three occasions while staggering to Calvary.
He is my model for persevering no matter how hard that is.

THE DEER

We live near some heavily forested areas, dense enough to provide dens for herds of deer. We often see these animals at the edge of the woods. In the spring, the stag and doe introduce their little fawns to life in proximity to humans. By summer, the family grows adventuresome and wanders closer to the apple trees in our orchard, seeking some tasty fruit. I often approach the deer slowly, avoiding any sudden movement. While instinctively wary, the animals will often let me get as close as twenty yards. They are magnificent creatures! To reach apples higher in the trees, the buck will sometimes stand on his hind legs; what a sight! All the while, the parents are carefully herding the children to keep them from harm's way. In the fall the young ones have grown to adult size. It is remarkable that the deer have such a basic impulse toward protecting their family, nurturing their offspring to maturity and repeating the cycle again and again. We humans can gain some important insight by observing these lovely animals.

As parents, then grandparents, we are concerned about our offspring, too. We strive to raise them with good values, provide a solid education and hope they will become productive and responsible adults. No matter how long they live, we still consider them to be our "kids." If we are wise, we will turn them over to God at some point. Have you done that?

God Who rules the natural world,
You have embedded natural family instincts in Your creatures.
Sometimes we humans unwisely cause family discord.
Help us all, Lord, to fulfill our family roles as You would wish.

CHARLIE AND JANE

I wrote previously that I volunteer as a hospital chaplain. On my rounds one day I entered Charlie's room; his wife, Jane, was at the bedside holding Charlie's hand. I'm not a doctor but I could see Charlie was near death. He was drifting in and out of consciousness, while Jane was quietly speaking words of love to him. I gently asked Jane what had happened. She told me they had fifty wonderful years together, and they had celebrated their Golden Anniversary with an ocean cruise. Until then, Charlie had not had a sick day in his life. Upon returning from their cruise just weeks ago, Charlie had a routine physical. It was determined he was full of cancer. This sudden health reversal had shocked them both, and now it was obvious Jane was about to become a widow. I began to offer some prayers for the dying:

> *"We know we have passed from death to life because we love each other..." (1 John 3:14)*

> *"Though I should walk in death's dark valley I fear no evil with You at my side." (Psalm 23:4)*

Both of them found comfort in these words. He weakly squeezed her hand and offered a faint smile. They had begun to say goodbye. It wasn't easy, but it was beautiful. I was lucky to share that moment with these two lovers and friends.

How do I feel about the inevitability of my own death? How will I react to the death of my closest loved ones? I'm not sure.

God, source of joyful life and mercy at death,
Physical death offers the ultimate finality for us all.
My faith says there is something wonderful beyond the veil.
Lord, I need courage to face that final breath. Help me!

THE "FIVE – FIFTY" PALATE

Folks having dinner in our lovely community dining room often share a bottle of wine. Most people purchase moderately priced bottles of very passable wine. Over time, I have postulated a theory about this modest imbibing. It goes like this: if you have a glass of wine from a bottle costing less than $5.00 retail, you can tell it is a marginal product; if you have a glass of wine from a bottle costing more than $50.00 retail, you know you are experiencing a very superior product. However, wine priced between $5.00 and $50.00 is often difficult to differentiate because many of us do not have discriminating palates. In that price range most wine tastes pleasantly the same. So, why over-spend on wine when your guests won't really appreciate the difference? Even if my theory is incorrect, it is a great way to rationalize the purchase of inexpensively priced wine to share. Do I sound cheap?

There are some life lessons in this theory. Throughout the day, I encounter many people and participate in lots of things. Some of these situations are pleasant; others are irritating or prickly. I must learn not to get too upset or overly enthusiastic about common events. I know I need to practice keeping an even keel, not letting things or people "get under my skin" or make me too euphoric. Developing a non-discriminating palate about life's daily events is a worthy goal.

God Who blesses us with calmness and consistency,
I wish my life did not have so many little ups and downs.
Please show me how to shrug off minor daily irritations.
Similarly, teach me to keep my enthusiasm under control.
Give me a spiritual palate that sees all as Your gifts to me.

MASSAGING OF HANDS

"Touch was never meant to be a luxury. It is a basic human need, an action that validates life while giving hope to both the receiver and the giver. The healing of touch is reciprocal." (Author unknown). Julia has organized a dozen women in the community to visit the skilled nursing and special needs units in our care center twice each month. The people there are either seriously ill or live with various forms of dementia. Julia and her friends offer hand massages, a gesture of loving kindness to virtual strangers. I am told by staff that the recipients of these massages are grateful and uplifted by this intimate service they receive. I can only imagine that those providing this charitable action obtain wonderful satisfaction by what they do for others. This seems to define a "win-win" situation, as our anonymous author said, "reciprocal healing."

Those offering the massages do not have special training or skills. Yet what they do is a profound act of compassion and concern for others. What kinds of things can I do to provide a similar level of comfort to others? The beauty of this story is the fact that mighty talent is not needed to give great service to our brothers and sisters. Even if you think of yourself as lacking any charism, what can you do to improve someone's life? Even the most humble have lots of things to offer.

Savior God, Who teaches us about compassion,
Show me simple things I can do to build up Your kingdom.
I think I must hit a home run each time I come up to bat.
No, You tell me, a simple bunt single will do just fine.
Like this baseball metaphor, show me how to win the game.
Victory is achieved when I do my part to help others.

CRATER LAKE

God provides the human race a glorious encounter with His creation at Crater Lake in southern Oregon. Those who visit often describe feeling a profound spiritual experience. Standing at a vantage point near the Lodge, the magnificent view takes away your breath. The color of the water mirrors the sky above. The surface of the lake seems like a giant sheet of deep blue glass. Projecting out of the lake is the mysterious, cone shaped Wizard Island. The caldera created by a former volcano embraces the water like a gorgeous, craggy and massive bowl almost two thousand feet above the water line. And the silence! Only the hum of industrious bees and the songs of birds break the utter stillness. No one can come here without having their spirit touched in some special way.

The remote location and nine months of deep snow prevents large numbers of people from visiting this natural wonder. Many can only dream of seeing such a magnificent place. Yet, all people aspire to uplifting experiences that touch and heal their souls. In my humdrum life, what places can I visit to find solitude, peace, renewal, gratitude, wisdom and grace? Not all can encounter Crater Lake, but all need such a place to discover the inner silence that all men and women crave.

Spirit God, our source of serenity and solitude,
You have blest me with several visits to awesome Crater Lake.
On each occasion I have come away with a soaring spirit.
I often search for a similar location in my daily life.
What place or person will duplicate the Crater Lake feeling?
Lord, teach me look for peace and love in everyday things.
Perhaps I will find these when I focus my search for You.

FALLING

Falling is the most dreaded curse of the elderly. Everyone in our retirement community takes inordinate precautions to avoid a fall. In spite of this, they occur with alarming regularity causing minor to very serious consequences. Falls are rarely anonymous; victims are observed the next day with crutches, walkers and canes while displaying garish purple blemishes around the face and on the arms. More serious incidents require paramedics, ambulances to the hospital and extended rehabilitation. Our wellness staff is forever teaching balance classes and offering strategies to defend against falling. My wife took a serious tumble while walking around our campus. Her injuries forced a 9-1-1 call, an ambulance ride and extended healing for a lacerated mouth and broken leg. Have you ever tried to use crutches when you're in your late seventies? Believe me—or my wife—it isn't easy to do.

I am reminded that falls are not just a physical occurrence. I can also experience emotional, spiritual and psychological stumbles, too. Everything seems great. I am happy and upbeat. Then, suddenly, a person snarls some very hurtful words that shatter my mood. Perhaps I unexpectedly enter an arid patch where my prayer life seems lacking in fervor. Life teaches me that I must deal with multiple types of falls. In each case, the first thing I must do is get up and try again.

God of mercy, slow to anger, rich in fidelity,
Please keep me safe from physical falls that injure my body.
Be gracious to me when I stumble in other ways, too.
Should I experience a fall from grace, help me to be reconciled.
Assist me in staying spiritually upright during all my days.

OUR PERSONAL SONG

One Sunday, Father Freddie from Uganda celebrated Mass in our chapel. His moving homily spoke about important traditions in his country. When a young woman becomes pregnant, she leaves her community and travels to a deserted place. It is only there that she can hear and learn the unique song being sung by the infant in her womb. Afterwards, she returns to her village and teaches the song to her neighbors so they can sing it to her child when it is born. When the child grows and is ready for marriage, the songs of both the bride and groom are sung at the wedding. Likewise, upon death, the person's song is chanted one final time in farewell. In Fr. Freddie's culture, each person has a distinctive song that follows that individual throughout life. I was very touched by this story. What a lovely idea; we each have a song for life, initially taught by us to our Mothers while we await our birth.

In my community, I frequently meet new people. They begin as strangers to me. Little by little, I learn more about them. Where were you born? What about your parents? Where were you educated? Do you have siblings? What was your career? Tell me about your interests and areas of accomplishment? Slowly, I learn their song—their story—and possibly they learn mine. Until I thoroughly know the words to my friend's song, I do not know them intimately. How can I honor them at special times if I don't know all the words and music to their song?

Triune God,
You are a community—Father, Son, Spirit.
Three Persons in one God is not a fact to be understood.
It is mysterious article of faith to be lived in my daily life.
Almighty God, help me to learn Your song so I may know You.

"WHY ME?"

A man in the hospital told me a frightening story. While working in his yard, he was bitten on his upper back by a spider. He wasn't overly concerned until he began to suffer serious symptoms about twenty-four hours later. He was rushed to the emergency room where doctors discovered the insect bite carried a flesh-eating virus. By the time treatment commenced, severe damage had been done directly above the man's spinal column. Only quick and massive medical intervention had saved him from a life-threatening event. His response: "Why me? How could a loving God give this insect such lethal power over a human being?" He wasn't through yet. "And, why would a loving God allow my wife to die from cancer two years ago? God is neither loving nor fair and has treated me harshly although I am blameless." He would not be consoled by a discussion of God's inscrutable plan for each of us. He was also not interested in Job's biblical story.

Have you ever said, "Why me?" I have, many times. Some misfortune befalls me. My immediate reaction is to cry out, "This is unfair! Let someone else bear this load." I have become angry with God for letting this happen to me. Can't He see that I am doing my best and don't deserve this burden? This is one of life's great unanswered questions: why do bad things happen to good people. How do *you* resolve this?

God Who has an unfathomable plan for each of us,
I accept this idea grudgingly because of my human frailty.
Your infinite majesty leaves me feeling distant from You.
I want to be close to You, embraced in Your loving arms.
Help me to accept what comes and see Your plan for my life.

REHABILITATION DONE TWICE

Ten years ago when my wife had a hip replaced, the surgery was quite complicated and the rehabilitation long and arduous. Now, procedures are simplified, the incision is quite small, much of the surgery is done robotically and rehabilitation is less strenuous. In spite of these advances, the operation is not trivial and post surgical therapy is still required. My friend Dick recently had his hip replaced. The surgery went well and within a couple of days he was feeling ready to return to his duties. He was lulled into a false sense of wellness believing that all the regimen of his prescribed therapy might not be necessary after all. You can probably guess what happened next. While exiting an auto, his repaired hip dislocated, causing him helplessness and extreme pain. He was taught a difficult lesson; there are no shortcuts to complete recovery especially after a serious operation. His lesson lasted six weeks and the teacher was a taskmaster about learning well the lessons being taught on the second try.

Consider the life lessons in this story. I am often confronted with tasks to complete, projects to finish or relationships to mend. Human nature tells me to look for the easy way or the path of least resistance so I can quickly remove this item from my "to do" list. Perhaps I will find a shorter route but usually the longer road must be traveled even with its potholes.

Spirit God, teacher of lessons both great and small,
I find myself always searching for shortcuts in life.
"There must be an easier, less difficult way," I think.
I quickly tire of extended effort, above all with relationships.
"No," the Spirit says, "be thorough, especially with love."

THE "ARAB SPRING"

An insignificant street vendor selling vegetables in Tunis was constantly hassled by low-level bureaucrats. One day, a government agent confiscated the vendor's scale for a minor infraction of rules. This was "the straw that broke the camel's back." Frantic with anger, the vendor expressed his raging frustration at this unfair treatment by soaking his body in gasoline and then immolating himself. This ghastly act initiated protests by citizens against brutal, monolithic leaders in Tunisia, Egypt, Yemen, Bahrain, Libya and Syria. Within weeks northern Africa and the mid-east were boiling with demonstrations and violent dissent against the countries' despotic rulers. Many of these nations had been ruled with iron fists for over forty years. The typical inhabitant had few rights, was treated harshly and subject to jail and execution without due process. The people said, "Enough!" Some tyrant leaders were overthrown and others were forced to expand the rights and economic opportunities for their citizens. This process is ongoing and the final outcome is in doubt. It is clear that a match lighted by a peasant started a massive conflagration, a fire that possibly cannot be quenched.

What have I done to right a serious wrong in society? Have I ever seen injustice, unfair or harsh treatment of the poor or marginalized members of our society—and done nothing?

God Who loves the poor and downtrodden,
I avoid getting involved in issues of social justice.
It is risky and inconvenient to stick out my neck for others.
What if I am criticized, scorned, or held up to ridicule?
Lord, give me courage to advocate for the less fortunate.

THE RESIDENT FUND

Some senior citizens are nervous about outliving their financial resources. Even with careful planning, their retirement nest eggs seem to shrink at an alarming rate. With folks living longer, many people could exhaust their money prior to their deaths. This idea is frightening to many. Addressing this problem, our retirement community created a fund to assist those with depleted resources. The Resident Fund may provide help to those who drain their funds through no fault of their own. This is done confidentially after careful scrutiny of the person's financial situation. Unfortunately, the size of the Fund is not large enough to help all those who may need it. Obtaining contributions is hard, frustrating work.

Why don't all of the more affluent residents cheerfully and generously contribute to the Resident Fund? There are many reasons offered: conservation of their own funds; a desire to leave inheritances; a sense of denial about the underlying problem or a natural human instinct to hoard in the event of a future shortage. Even though they are kind and good in most respects, it is difficult to get these well-to-do people to donate to the worthy cause supported by the Resident Fund. Am I sufficiently generous to those who could use my assistance? How much should be considered enough to give? I don't know.

God Who loves the generous and cheerful giver,
I constantly dither about my gifts to worthwhile charities.
Do I selfishly amass and squirrel away my assets?
Am I a Midas with my money, always needing a bigger cache?
How will I be judged, Lord, about sharing what I have?
Help me to see that generosity is really about trust in You.

WAXING THE CAR

Jim and Patty operate a small business detailing automobiles. They prepare new cars for many dealers and also handle retail customers like me. I have used their services for many years. It's amazing how grimy, greasy and dull a car can become even when it's garaged and occasionally taken to a car wash. I'm always pleased when I retrieve my car after it has been professionally washed, cleaned and waxed. Every surface is like showroom new, in and out. The leather seats and trim have a buttery feel and the metal skin has a silky finish and appearance. It's almost like acquiring a new car once a year. Driving home, I imagine my vehicle is going faster and getting better gas mileage because there is less wind resistance!

In some respects I am like my automobile. Even though I attempt to regularly nurture my spiritual life, I find my soul can become smudged and dreary too. How can this happen? Once so full of good intentions, moral resolve and spiritual purpose, I discover a gray, soiled conscience, rough relationships and a tepid prayer life. Just like my car, I need an occasional rejuvenation. A short retreat, a simple day of recollection or immersion in a good spiritual book often does the trick. What have you done that works for you?

God of spiritual re-birth for us all,
I frequently find myself spiritually off track. St. Paul said,
"The good I would do, I do not do; The evil I would not do, I do."
When I find myself on the wrong spiritual path, Help me, Lord, to
rejuvenate myself.

WAR STORIES

My retirement community has a large glass display cabinet. Every couple of months a committee fills the cupboard with items of interest loaned by the residents. Recently the display centered on military memorabilia, things like medals, emblems and war souvenirs. Included were Bronze Stars, Purple Hearts and Distinguished Service Crosses. Many of the residents were genuine heroes during World War II and Korea. At the conclusion of the exhibit cycle, a group gathered to hear the personal stories of those who had contributed items to the display. Several men told of their experiences in a humble, self-effacing manner. They described their exploits as nothing at all. Any successes achieved were mostly called "lucky breaks." To the rest of us it was apparent we were in the presence of greatness. These men spent years in harm's way, were very courageous and sacrificed much for their fellow citizens. In day-to-day contacts, these fellows seem quite ordinary, possessing no special attributes—just average human beings. The achievements and bravery of their youth tell a different story. I feel privileged to call them neighbors.

Have I ever done courageous or brave acts? Do I ever puff up the stories to make myself look important or special? What character traits do these war heroes possess that permits them to minimize their own greatness while telling their stories? I would like to emulate them in my own life.

Spirit God, Who provides the grace to do our duty,
Help me to be resolute and always try to do the right thing.
I am often presented with difficult choices in my daily life.
Teach me that I can always turn to You for needed courage.

FAMILY VISITS

A visit with one of our six children and their family is a special occasion for my wife and me. Only one family is nearby. The rest are scattered so we don't see them as often. It is a great treat to visit with the grandchildren. Many are now teenagers and they are growing so fast. It seems like only yesterday when family visits were devoted to diaper changing and feeding babies. Now, we are enjoying adult conversations with maturing young men and women. What a transformation! Our interaction with our kids and their spouses is equally anticipated. We get caught up with their professional lives, what is going on in their homes, neighborhoods and churches. We divide our clan into "Hadleys" and "Hadnotleys," teasingly separating those who were born into our family from those who married into it. No one has taken offense at the moniker assigned to their non-Hadley status. At least, not yet.

We try to get everyone together once a year. What an event that is! Non-stop talking, eating and a variety of activities suck up the time available like a vacuum. These annual reunions have defined our family for the past twenty-five years. The get-togethers are called "Camp Hadley – a family sharing love."

Sadly, we know friends who have estranged family members. Years pass without contact or any expression of concern. What can possibly wound the heart more than alienated family?

God Who blesses love between family members,
Help me to maintain good relations with all my relatives.
Our family tree bonds all of us together in good times and bad.
Let me strive for unconditional love even in times of conflict.

SPEND WISELY

Have you seen this one on the Internet? I think it is worth revisiting since it conveys a powerful message to all of us.

"Imagine that you won the following prize in a contest. Each morning, your bank would receive a deposit for your account totaling $86,400. The contest has only three simple rules: any funds you didn't spend during the next 24 hours would be taken away from you; next, you may not transfer any of the money to another account; finally, the contest could be ended at any time without notice and your account would be closed. What would you do? Probably you would buy everything you ever wanted. You would also lavish money on your family, friends, worthwhile causes and even strangers since you couldn't possibly spend it all on yourself. Actually, this contest is reality. Each of us possesses a magical bank account— not of money but *time*. Yes, each new day we are given 86,400 seconds as a gift of life. This time may be more valuable than an equivalent amount of dollars. We don't get to save any seconds for the next day. Yesterday is gone forever. Our account can be closed at any time without warning. So, what will you do with the 86,400 seconds given to you today? Enjoy every second of your life since time passes more quickly than we can imagine. Be good to yourself, take care of your neighbor, love deeply and be thankful for the time you have."

Infinite God Who always was and always will be,
Teach me to be grateful for the finite time I have been given.
Show me how to use each moment for kindness and love.
Spending time wisely doesn't require non-stop activity.
Instruct me how to enjoy quiet solitude to hear Your voice.

PASTOR KEN

Ken is the Pastor of a vibrant Protestant church. During the fifteen years I have known him, I've seen Ken develop from an enthusiastic young minister into a formidable churchperson of great stature. Actually, I consider Ken to be a modern day St. Paul. Ken's intensely focused objective is to bring the love of Jesus Christ to as many people as he can. To accomplish this, Ken has founded many new churches in America as well as foreign countries, often installing ministers he has personally trained. Although he has affected thousands of lives in the world, Ken has never sought the status or wealth of many who lead large congregations. He remains a simple, friendly, humble and dedicated pastor to his flock. He claims no special talent or spiritual vision but he has shrewdly marshaled financial resources to accomplish his unwavering goal of expanding God's kingdom here on earth. This has been done during many personal trials. Ken is an inspiration to me. Dare I already refer to him as St. Kenneth? He would be amused.

How often do I wait for someone more talented or specially gifted to accomplish some task? Another person would surely be more qualified than me to take on a project and see it to completion. I don't have enough time, energy or skill to offer. Too often I fall back on the old saying: "Let George do it."

God Who loves the poor in spirit and humble of heart,
Show me that I have been given unique gifts to use.
I must learn to step forward even when I feel inadequate.
Moses avoided leading. Jonah objected. Ananias was terrified.
Let me feel Your hand on my shoulder when it is my turn.
Lord, keep the promise You made to Moses: "I will be with you."

ECONOMIC ILLITERACY

To the average person or household, day-to-day economics is pretty simple. Over the long haul, one must have reliable income that exceeds periodic expenses. Occasionally there will be purchases of large items (houses, cars, etc.) or emergency expenses that must be financed by loans or with credit cards. Everyone knows that these borrowed sums plus interest must eventually be repaid. The amounts required for repayment must be included in the normal periodic expenses. It's all quite understandable, actually. Failure to follow this very basic formula can cause terrible stress, anxiety and personal pain and may even result in bankruptcy or financial ruin. How is it our civic leaders can't figure this out? For years now, our government has spent more than it has collected then borrowed to make up the difference. We face huge annual deficits and have amassed an unfathomable national debt. Why has this crisis occurred? I offer the following explanation. Because it sounds so complicated, I think the average citizen doesn't believe that simple rules apply to government. The numbers are so large, the programs so complex, and the tax code so unintelligible that we have become economic illiterates. Is this too harsh an assessment? We must figure out a solution to this serious problem—quickly—or all of us will be adversely affected and our country forced into economic decline.

God Who has given us free will to make choices,
I am overwhelmed by the problems facing my country.
Equity is important, balance is needed, but choices are hard.
How do we provide for the needy and vulnerable?
Simultaneously, how do we encourage economic growth?
Lord, send Your Spirit to bless our leaders with wisdom.

WILLAMETTE SHORE TROLLEY

In my town, we have an antique trolley (circa 1935) that goes back and forth to the Portland waterfront during the summer months. It is a most popular tourist attraction. The right-of-way features views of very beautiful homes, passage through tunnels, and rides over high trestles while traveling adjacent to the Willamette River much of the way. For two years, I was a volunteer motorman charged with preparing the trolley for the daily runs and also operating the train while providing a running narrative to my passengers. It was really fun, but also a lot of hard work. Since the car was quite old, we often had mechanical problems, so I felt the burden of responsibility to insure the trolley was operated safely for the benefit of the passengers, many of whom were little children. I was especially attracted to this volunteer service because I often rode similar streetcars as a boy in my hometown of Minneapolis. Being the motorman gave me a sense of *déjà vu* as I recalled the trolley rides of my youth. What memories!

As I age, I make increasing reference to "the good old days." Why do I often believe that things past were better than things present? I cite manners, courtesy, public discourse, and moral values where the past seems better than the present. Why do I seemingly ignore the advances of the current time? Have you experienced this same distortion of mind yourself?

God Who always was, always is and always will be,
I find that nostalgia for things long past often rules my life.
Unconsciously, I love the past but distrust the present.
The past is gone, the future not yet; I must live this moment.
Teach me to value the here and now. It's where I find You.

MY MONTHLY LOG

Since 1986, I have written a monthly log, or diary. At the end of each month, I prepare a summary of what has happened in my life, at least those things I believe are noteworthy. While re-reading the log, I find that most of the record is quite boring, lacks much writing flair and is of interest to a precious few. I do hope that perhaps one hundred years from now, some relative will discover my dusty notebooks in an old box and enjoy this pedestrian history report of one ancestor's life experiences. The future reader will find details about my daily life, people I interacted with, local and world events and my view of the political and economic situation at the moment. Over time, one will find the soaring highs, depressing lows, excitement and the ordinariness of life. There are stories of triumph, loss, pain, happiness, mistakes, pleasure, anger and love. You can discover heroes, villains, saints and sinners all in lower case. Over twenty-five years, I find that all the stories are different and yet the same. I might even like to come back in the next century and re-read this log myself. Do you take time to keep any records of your life?

Journaling is often suggested as a way to deepen your spiritual life. Writing down the ways in which we encounter God, deal with our human failings and problems and strengthen our prayer life is said to be a helpful tool. Is this something you might consider doing in your own life?

God Who inspires us to know, love and serve You,
How do I get in touch with my spiritual nature?
Show me how to be a caring person and neighbor to all.
With Your help, I can be better, pray deeply, love earnestly.

THE SURGERIES

I recently had my fourth surgical procedure. I was pretty lucky; I had not been admitted to a hospital until I was sixty-eight years old. This story is not about my operations; how boring would that be? The interesting part is the tremendous advances hospitals have made during the last decade in their surgical departments. Everything has changed! Paper is obsolete; all the records are kept on computers. Pre-surgical nursing care is more thorough and extensive. They have learned that keeping the patient warm before going to the operating room results in a faster exit from anesthetic, less infection and quicker healing. The operations are often shorter because of robotic tools and the three-dimensional views seen by the surgeons of the area to be repaired or replaced. Except for the most difficult and invasive operations, the patient is up and walking as soon as possible. After my most recent back surgery, I walked extensively within four hours after leaving the operating room...amazing! Most of you would agree that hospitals are no fun, but surgical procedures are easier now.

Hospitals work to better themselves. Shouldn't I try to do the same? What have I done to improve my relationships with families, friends and neighbors in the last decade? Do I make it a habit to read books or attend lectures about dealing with personal improvement? Do you think this applies to you, too?

God Who graces those in the medical profession,
I need the same blessings to improve my relations with others.
Often I am satisfied with my status in life; why change things?
I believe things are going pretty well; adjustments are a bother.
*Teach me, Lord, an important lesson: **good enough never is.***

51

OUR FAMILY FLAG

I wrote previously about "Camp Hadley"—our annual family reunion. We have been doing this for twenty-five years. Part of the tradition revolved around the design and production of a family flag. Each household has a copy. It is rectangular. The left side is green, the right side white. There is a large blue circle in the center of the flag containing a white "H" and six white stars. The green denotes our Irish heritage. The white symbolizes optimism. The royal blue circular canton speaks to an unbroken ring of support for each other and the color denotes love. The six bright stars are for the families in the clan. The "H" is for Hadley. The flag is flown when we have one of our reunions and, as the instructions call for, "other special occasions." It's a fun thing.

It has turned out to be fun...but more than that. As the grandchildren came along, they were taught that their family relationships were important, and that we must love, be loyal and support one another. Each part of the flag tells about these values, historical facts or what the "elders" consider a significant part of our extended family. It has been a great way to pass on the meaning of family love. Do you have similar traditions within your extended family?

Jesus, Mary and Joseph who constitute the Holy Family,
I ask that you bless every person in our family tree.
Not just our relatives, Lord, but all households in the world.
Send special love to those who have no family to share with.
They have a particular need of Your warm, loving embrace.

THE FARMERS' MARKET

In downtown Lake Oswego, we have an expansive city park adjacent to the municipal lake. On Saturday mornings in May through October, a market is conducted that is full of delicious local fruits and vegetables, baked goods, arts and crafts and places to purchase food of all kinds. The market is packed and parking is difficult. But, everyone comes because the selection of goods and services is so appealing. Frequently, there is also some type of entertainment so people are also attracted to hear a local band, laugh at a comic or wonder at a juggler or magician. As young people say, "This is a happening place!" The people attending the Farmers' Market are as diverse as the products offered for sale. Young couples pushing strollers, middle-aged folks stocking up on nutritious food and older people having breakfast while enjoying the sunny, warm day amid the hustle and bustle. It is an all-together attractive scene, probably replicated in many places around the country during the spring and summer months.

These wonderful opportunities for civic social interaction between citizens are largely taken for granted. I don't think most of us appreciate the freedom we have to assemble, to choose what we want to consume and be kept safe by our local police force. How fortunate we are to live in the United States.

God Who has blessed this country so abundantly,
Let me never forget to praise You for Your wonderful gifts.
Oceans, east and west, with great rivers and lakes between.
Snow-capped mountains and golden plains offer their beauty.
Complacency is the greatest threat we face in today's world.
Teach me never to neglect thanking You for these blessings.

MARYLHURST UNIVERSITY

Our retirement community is located on the same contiguous plot of ground as Marylhurst University. The school was founded in 1893 as a women's college. Through the years, Marylhurst has become a broad-based university with a student population of adults having an average age of thirty-five years. It is not overstatement to say the university is thriving and has a reputation for offering creative courses of study designed to accommodate the working student. There are also many programs directed to those in our community. Lectures, concerts, Shakespearian plays and other cultural events are always being announced on our bulletin boards. Special arrangements can be made for us seniors to audit Marylhurst classes for a nominal fee. It is really interesting to speak with someone in our community who has taken Muslim history or a course on writing or music. People in their eighties and nineties return to our campus energized and invigorated. Marylhurst is beautifully situated on the banks of the Willamette and makes a perfect place for an early evening stroll, too. It is wonderful to have the university so close by.

As a youth, I couldn't wait for school to end each year. Now aged, I see the value of lifetime continuing education. Some say when we stop learning we stop living. I am going to avoid that trap. How do you feel about more education for yourself?

God Who wondrously provided us with intellect,
Let me see the value of keeping my mind vital and alert.
While our bodies deteriorate, our minds can be kept in tune.
Show me that I contribute to society when I am educated.
Lord, help me to persevere when more study seems tedious.

REPENT: CHANGE YOUR MIND

I have been told that the most frequently seen word in the New Testament is "repent." I am also informed that the best literal Hebrew translation for repent is "to change your mind." John the Baptist, the herald to Jesus Christ, spent his public life preaching a life of repentance to all. John would shout to his followers, "Repent! The kingdom of God is at hand!" I thought John meant that people should stop doing evil things and return to a life of loving God and neighbor. Apparently, I had that wrong. The Baptist was telling people to change the way they thought about things. What things? I am not a Bible scholar so my ideas about mind-changing may be at odds with the recognized scripture experts. Here are some of my thoughts about John's preaching: "The Messiah you expect is not going to be a military leader, but a spiritual one." " Don't get hung up on all your laws; without love there is no law;" "The Savior is coming; make a straight, not crooked, path for Him."

I have many ideas about how things should be. I am not interested in changing my mind about most of them. I will happily tell you everything you need to know about politics, religious beliefs, how to play baseball correctly, ethical standards, or how to cook a steak. If John the Baptist had lived in my time he probably would have said to me, "You're going to have to abandon some of your rigid thinking."

God Who has provided us with a guide for our lives,
Help me to see the foolishness of opinionated thinking.
When I have all the answers, I don't understand the questions.
I rely too much on my own ideas but I'm not open to others.
Lord, make me malleable so that I will accept needed change.

FLAG DAY

We have an active Boy Scout troop in our neighborhood. On Flag Day, and all the other national holidays, these boys come by early and decorate the common areas of our retirement community with American flags. It is good to get up and see The Stars and Stripes displayed so prominently around our campus. To those of us who lived through World War II, Korea or Viet Nam seeing Old Glory wave provides a deep patriotic experience. It is no longer, "My country right or wrong," but the flag does remind us how fortunate we are to live in this blessed place even with all its faults and failings. I hear all the complaints about our politics, injustice in our social services, gaps between the rich and poor, environmental indifference and racial inequality. But where else would you or I prefer to live? Can you think of one place that offers political, religious or economic freedom, gender equality or the opportunity to reach your full potential that compares to the United States? I cannot. So long may our flag wave over the land of the free and the home of the brave. And, special blessings on the Boy Scouts who remind me throughout the year how fortunate I am to live in this land that has been blessed by God.

Somehow, "patriotism" became a dirty word during the past ten years. Some call it a code word for attacks on diversity and multiculturalism in our society. I don't agree. To be patriotic says I love my country and I'm proud to live here—period.

God Who loves all people and blesses all lands,
Let me be proud of my country without denigrating others.
Teach me that Your unconditional love crosses all borders.
Lord, let me feel the equality of all men throughout the earth.

A SUNDAY AFTERNOON DRIVE

Do you remember as a kid when your father, or another relative, took your family on a Sunday afternoon drive? It was exciting to get away from the cheek-by-jowl houses in your neighborhood and make a leisurely trip to visit a nearby park, lake, a relative's farm or scenic site. Oregon is a wonderful place for this activity. In the Portland area, we have an Urban Growth Boundary, a program designed to contain community sprawl. I can leave a concrete and asphalt neighborhood and soon I'm traveling on two lane rural roads, seeing rail fences guarding rolling meadows that are filled with beautiful fir, alder, cedar and birch trees plus wildflowers and animals of all kinds. Views from the crests of the valleys west of the Cascade Mountains offer spectacular yet tranquil vistas of the valley floor and Mt. Hood, Mt. Jefferson and Mt. St. Helens in the eastern and northern directions. Pulling over to the side of the road and gazing over these sights can transform a person's sense of well being in a magical way. This is easy to do in a beautiful place like Oregon where I am privileged to reside.

How did I lose sight of the plain delights available to me in everyday life? Strolling through a park, watching the sunset from a spot on a beach or observing hummingbirds feeding on lush summer flowers cost me nothing and yet are priceless. Are you like me, wishing you could unhook yourself from the non-stop noise that our modern culture defines as pleasure?

God Who offers a universe full of simple pleasures,
Let me discover organic bliss and disconnect faux diversions.
Help me to find my true leisure in all the wonders of nature.
Bless me with joy that is found in the real, not artificial, world.

THE CONSUMER SOCIETY

Richard John Neuhaus, a great Catholic theologian, wrote:

Consumerism is not simply the state of being well off. It is the spiritual disposition of being controlled by what one consumes, of living in order to consume, of living in order to have things. This, of course, is a great spiritual danger for rich and poor alike.

Who could effectively argue that we do not reside in a consumer society, especially in the western industrialized countries? Even the least affluent live on "smart" phones, get their entertainment on flat screen plasma televisions and cruise the Internet on the most up-to-date laptops driven by sophisticated software systems. As Fr. Neuhaus says, many of us are controlled by what we consume, actually exist to consume and have more of virtually everything. He makes a further interesting point: this mind-set poses a spiritual menace for everyone in society. If it is true that things control us, then we have lost the power to control ourselves.

How have I permitted this to happen in my life? When did I become obsessed with possessing every material thing made by man? Even if I have avoided total surrender to the consumer world, I am not merely an innocent bystander. I am frightened by my impotence in the face of consumerism.

God of all things on the earth,
Please help me realize the perils of obsessive consumption.
I gorge myself with trifles in my voracious quest for more.
Nothing seems to satisfy my compulsive need to acquire.
Lord, succor my weakness and teach me moderation of desire.

GARDEN BOXES

Our retirement community provides garden boxes for those who still hanker to have some fruits, vegetables or flowers of their own. The boxes are 4' by 4' and are raised to about waist high. Each box allows the would-be farmer the opportunity to grow a couple of tomato plants, some chives, parsley, lettuce and squash, or a container full of spring and summer flowers. To those who maintained a garden at their homes, this offers a way to continue a pleasant diversion. Like any garden, the boxes require spring soil amendments, watering during the summer and protection from predators in the area, especially deer. My wife and I maintained one of these boxes for several years, but I suffer from a very un-green thumb so our ratio of output to effort expended was extremely low. Still, it is fun to watch your plantings grow and have a few deliciously fresh tomatoes, some butter lettuce and crisp cucumbers for an August lunchtime salad. I never figured out why some of my neighbors were so successful with their gardens and I wasn't.

It is easy to see that all people have unique gifts. Whether it's gardening, wood working, auto repair, playing a musical instrument, conducting a meeting—or a host of other things—some folks seem to outshine the rest of us with their effortless skills. I need to remember that they are thinking the same thing when they look at me. Do you know your singular gifts?

God Who blesses everyone with inimitable charisms,
Let me humbly accept the gifts and talents loaned to me.
Teach me that these blessings are to be used, not hidden.
When I fail to value my gifts, show me that this is false pride.
Lord, inspire me to utilize my ability in service to the world.

NORWAY MOURNS

Just two months short of ten years since September 11, 2001, the world stands in frozen horror once again. A massive bomb in downtown Oslo and the slaughter of scores of young people at a nearby youth camp represent a further incomprehensible act by a lunatic killer. Our friends, Inger and Chuck, live in Oslo. Following are excerpts from their email to us sent two days after the tragedy took place.

"We are safe but shaken and chilled by the events...This tragedy started years earlier in the head of the killer... He grew up in a system with freedom to think, act and do without regard to consequences...He has never known hunger, pain, anguish or poverty...He was encouraged by the State to participate in the political process...That is why this tragedy has shocked the nation. It is unbelievable that a real Norwegian could do this! We thought, 'surely this must be the work of a 'non-ethnic person'... There is great national anxiety about being called racist or uncaring...But our population is now almost 25% foreign...None of us was really prepared to deal with the realities of multiculturalism. We are all so conflicted by our feelings...We're afraid this event has changed our view of life in this beautiful, rich and generous country forever...That is truly sad."

I can read between the lines of this communication. I don't find fury, rage, or lust for revenge—only broken hearts. And now comes the hardest part: God tells me to love my enemies and do good to those who hate me. How can I possibly do this?

God Who offers unconditional love to each individual,
I find it pretty easy to be loving and forgiving to some.
They're just like me; I can overlook their occasional failings.
But what of those others, Lord, the ones who hate me?
Must I love them, too, in spite of their indifference to my pain?
Yes, says the Lord. Love of neighbor is non-negotiable with Me.

THE TREASURE TROVE

Located in a large public room in our retirement community a number of residents industriously manage a flea market known as the Treasure Trove. The proceeds from this operation are contributed to our Resident Fund that I wrote about previously. I am always amazed at the level of activity going on at this store. People are constantly donating small items and knick-knacks that can be sold. The committee prices the items and they are carefully displayed to obtain the best exposure. Finally, the large buyer group swoops in daily on the lookout for a trinket, candle stick, *demitasse* cup and saucer or some other little item that would be "just perfect" for a special spot in their apartment. So, what is really going on here? There are three distinct things rolled up in this one endeavor. First, running this little store provides significant social interaction among the workers. It's a great way to know your neighbors better and create lasting personal relationships. Second, the group encounters a shared experience of pulling together for a common good. Finally, the end product expands the Resident Fund so more people can be helped. Each of these outcomes enhances our community.

What do you and I do to improve the communities where we live? Are we willing to pull together so that $1 + 1 = 3$? As Thomas Dunne wrote, "No man is an island entire of himself."

God Who loves people of every nation, gender and race,
Show me how cooperative energy exceeds individual effort.
Help me understand the benefit of everyone pulling together.
Too often I delude myself that only I can get something done.
But when we join hands, our power for good multiplies.

LOCAL THEATRE

A short distance from our home is a building housing a local performance art theatre. The productions are heavily subscribed and the quality of shows is generally superb. In addition to a marvelous U-shaped theatre, there are several rehearsal studios and classrooms where aspiring performers can receive training. The props, lighting and staging are all first rate. The whole operation is a micro version of an "on Broadway" playhouse. The shows are diverse; we get to see drama, musicals, comedies and *avant-garde* productions. The cast is often sprinkled with professional actors so there is seldom a mediocre show. We really feel fortunate to have such high quality theatre so close and convenient to our home.

As a young person, I never saw myself as much of an actor. I didn't have the basic skills needed to be a performer. Later on I discovered that I was a terrific actor. I built elaborate devices around myself to make sure that people only saw what I wanted them to see. I became fascinated with a book written by a Jesuit priest entitled, "Why Am I Afraid to Tell You Who I Am?" To keep others from finding the darker side of my persona, I created some well-planned security. I also learned that I was not the only one doing this. Most people were acting similarly and creating their own defenses. I may still be afraid to let you know who I am. How about you?

All-knowing God Who sees into the depths of every soul,
What if my loved ones and friends knew everything about me?
I don't want them to know of my dark side and secrets.
What if they no longer loved or liked me? I couldn't bear it.
I need to overcome my vulnerability and become trusting.

THE WELLNESS CENTER; "THE GYM"

One of the busiest places in our community is the Wellness Center, referred to as "the gym." Full of state-of-the-art aerobic and resistance training machines, the gym gets busy about 5:30 AM and stays occupied by residents until the evening. Supplementing individual workouts, the staff frequently conducts classes and group activities, attempting to keep many residents fit for as long as possible. In addition to the equipment there is also a pool used for daily water aerobics and exercise programs. Many in their nineties are active participants in wellness activities. Still, there are some in the community who resist getting involved. The wellness staff is always thinking up ways to lure the unmotivated into the gym or pool. In most cases this is a very hard sell. Reasons not to exercise are legion and have been well honed over the years.

While not judging those who do not maintain their bodies, I believe we all have a duty to preserve a minimum level of general fitness. God gave each of us our amazing body; even when it becomes old, creaky and tired, we are called upon to keep it tuned up as best we can. I don't want to obsess over fitness, but feel I am called to cooperate with God's gift to me. I understand that certain people can no longer participate in fitness programs, but that does not excuse me from trying. How about you? Is some fitness routine part of your life?

Generous God Who co-created my magnificent body,
Motivate me to consistently follow a fitness program.
I need Your help when I am reluctant or feeling unwell.
My body is such a gift to me; show me how to care for it.
Please, Lord; help me to always appreciate Your generosity.

63

THE END OF THE OREGON TRAIL

Just a few miles from our home is the spot traditionally believed to be the end of the Oregon Trail. Consider the bravery of those who traveled the 2,000 miles from Missouri to Oregon City between 1834 and 1860. Those settling in Oregon amounted to over 53,000. Another 20,000 (estimated) died during the journey, which took about 160 days for initial trips. Can you imagine what was going through the minds of the men, women and children as they climbed onto the covered wagons to begin this trek? Emotions of fear, excitement, separation from loved ones, danger, hope and apprehension must have flooded over them as they headed west. Initially the pioneers had no way of knowing how this would all turn out. I am uncertain that I would have been willing to take the risks these courageous people faced.

Perhaps you can pin down your heritage to these pioneers. I cannot. In my earthly life, I have traced some of my ancestors back several hundred years. I frequently think about what kind of lives they lived and which of their genes have passed on to me. On the religious side, I know the exploits of my ancestors all the way back to the time of Christ—and before. Again, I find heroes, martyrs, great intellects and the most common of people—all building God's kingdom long before I arrived on the scene. My faith is meaningless without them.

Eternal God Who created my ancestors in history,
Pass on to me their courageous spirit and optimism.
My human predecessors have shaped my mind and body.
Those who preceded me in faith have left a spiritual legacy.
I honor their heritage while I shape the future for others.

VISITING THE MARIE ROSE CENTER

Part of our retirement community is devoted to the care of the frail elderly, the sick and those requiring special care because of dementia in some form. These folks live in a place called the Marie Rose Center. Those requiring some extra help with daily living chores live in Friendship Place, the assisted living area. Others who need skilled nursing care reside in Villa Marie. The special care/memory unit is named Caritas House. About one hundred people live in the Marie Rose Center. Those of us currently living independently know that we may need these extra levels of care one day. It is very comforting to have these wonderful, caring places available when we may require them. In the meantime, there is a steady stream of visitors to the Marie Rose Center from the rest of the campus. A smile, small bouquet of flowers or just simple conversation can lift the spirits of those experiencing deteriorating health of one kind or another. Each visitor thinks, "There, but for the grace of God, go I." I am quite sure it will be my turn one day to greet visitors calling upon me.

Compassion for others. How do I demonstrate this virtue? I try to show empathy to those experiencing difficulties and do what I can to alleviate their sadness or suffering. I must often examine my motivation and feelings for others. While I cannot console the world, I must reach out to comfort those I can.

Loving God, source of all compassion for those in stress,
Teach me how to offer sincere and loving care to the needy.
Sometimes I wince when I observe the afflictions of others.
I know that their sufferings today could be mine tomorrow.
Let me be like Simon, helping to carry another's cross.

STRIVING

(Adapted from a homily delivered by Fr. Richard Berg CSC in the Mary's Woods Chapel.) I think I have spent virtually my entire life in "striving mode." As a youngster I tried hard to become a good student and make my mom proud of me. I also did my best to improve my skills at baseball so I could play at higher levels as I grew up. College brought more struggles to excel in the classroom and be popular with other students. Military service required more attempts to be the best officer I could be. Marriage and family life demanded consistent endeavor to become a good husband, father and breadwinner. My career forced me to try very hard to be increasingly successful. Finally, in retirement, I attempt to be a good neighbor, a cheerful and helpful companion to my wife and a wise counselor to my children and grandchildren. Striving, struggling, endeavoring to do more—this seems to be a consistent pattern and direction for my life's journey.

When does this striving stop? At what point do I accept the fact that I am who I am, things are not going to change much despite my efforts and my sphere is pretty well settled? What I really must do is to unwind in the warm embrace of a God who loves me unconditionally just the way I am. Yes, I have done my best to be a good steward of the material possessions and gifts that have been loaned to me by God. Now, I am called to be calm, turn the final chores over to God and relax. Have you reached this point yet on your life's journey?

God Who teaches us to accept things the way they are,
I seem hard-wired to seek new challenges or hills to climb.
There is anxiety and unease over tasks left unaccomplished.
No matter how I try, my "to do" lists grow and do not diminish.
Lord, teach me to lighten up, take a break, let go and let God.

DINING WITH NEIGHBORS

The prime social event of the day revolves around neighbors in our community joining together to share the evening meal. In the formal Mt. Hood Dining Room or the casual Bistro Café, groups of residents are found interacting and enjoying one another's company while having their dinner. It is important that the food is good—and it is generally very appetizing—but that is only a portion of the dining experience. Residents getting to know one another better, sharing information about their lives, both present and past, trading amusing little stories—this is the essence of the social interaction between friends. There are often "small world" discoveries; people may learn about common places of birth, school attendance or prior employment in the same company. Folks who appear quite ordinary tell nonchalant tales about some of their achievements in life that mark them as most extraordinary. Governors, bridge builders, scientists, doctors, nurses, teachers at every level, business executives, lawyers, and entrepreneurs—all share the common experience of living in our retirement community. What a blessing it is to know them!

Until I moved here I didn't realize the benefit of meeting new people each day. All of us living here are normally distributed under a Bell Shaped Curve. That means there are a handful of weird folks at each end of the curve, but the majority are grouped in the middle. Isn't that true of your neighbors, too?

God Who gives each person unique talents and gifts,
Help me to be truly interested in others and learn from them.
Let me humbly admire the charisms You have loaned to them.
I see, Lord, that every person is superior to me in some way.

INTERFAITH CELEBRATIONS COMMITTEE

Mary's Woods Retirement Community is owned by an order of Catholic nuns. Interestingly, less than one-third of the residents claim to be Catholics. Since people of all faith heritage and belief are welcomed, honored and respected, there is an active Interfaith Celebrations Committee that plans religious events around some national and religious holidays. The programs are inspiring, touching and centered on prayer, scripture and spiritual hymns. We have several retired Protestant clergy living here and their participation is always welcomed. As Dean Inge (1860-1954) wrote, "It is impossible for those who mix at all with their fellowmen to believe that the grace of God is distributed denominationally."[1] The hand of God works through Catholics, Protestants, Jews and those of all faiths. The vibrancy of our Interfaith Celebrations Committee shows us this is so.

[1] *From "Living With Christ" August 2011 Issue.*

I can be righteous about my religion and the teachings of my church. I often believe my co-religionists and I are the only ones who possess the truth. Then I encounter some God-fearing, spiritual person of a different religion who is obviously in love with both the Creator and his neighbor. Isn't God working through this person, too? Am I the only one in relationship with the Lord because of my faith? I don't think so. Do you agree that God works through other faiths, too?

God Who offers salvation to all having a sincere heart,
Teach me that I do not have exclusive rights to God's truth.
Jesus founded my church, but His Spirit is available to all.
Instead of arguing about creeds, I should pray for unity.
Lord, teach me to join with others who seek You earnestly

THE CHRISTMAS RECEPTION

At Christmastime, the Sisters living in our community host a reception for all the other residents. Their Community Room is festively decorated, and you will find hot apple cider, delicious savory foods, cookies, candies and cakes of all kinds. I often tease the Sisters about what wonderful cooks they are. Most of them are quick to tell me that they are especially good at opening boxes from Costco and popping the contents in the oven. Several nuns will also open their apartments for a "tour." They love to show off their abundant holiday decorations and the modest living units they call home. For new residents this is often their first personal encounter with Sisters; the non-Catholics, in particular, come away charmed by the gracious hospitality offered by the nuns. Everyone who shows up is sincerely welcomed with big smiles, a plate of food and drink and pleasant conversation. This reception is a major highlight of the Christmas season.

What's the big deal? It's just another holiday party, right? No, this party is different; it offers sincere hospitality. One of the hallmarks of a committed Christian is friendliness towards others, especially strangers. Warmth, kindness and a generous welcome makes a statement from one person to another: "God loves you and I love you, too." Wouldn't the world be better if I treated everyone in that fashion?

Tender God Who offers loving hospitality to all people,
Teach me the importance of displaying kindness to everyone.
I cannot influence them unless they believe I am their friend.
Warmth, generosity and respect count more than my words.
Lord, help me to treat others with love, especially strangers.

CONCERTS IN THE CHAPEL

We often have musical performances in our beautiful chapel. The acoustics are pretty good, many can be seated comfortably, and the steps leading up to the altar provide a platform where the performers can be seen by the audience. Sometimes we have a single pianist. We are also entertained by small chamber music groups and larger ensembles. Many in our community have special appreciation for classical music. Others, like me, lack musical knowledge but enjoy watching and hearing the talented performers. The old saying, "Music has charms to soothe the savage breast," is quite apt. What can be more calming than beautiful melodies coming from a violin, classical guitar or grand piano? I am not really bothered by my cultural inadequacy. The exquisite sound of the music being produced is my reward even if I don't know much about the composer, relevant background information or the history of the piece being performed. Maybe I should attend nearby Marylhurst University and take a music appreciation course. I'm confident that would be a worthwhile investment of time.

All of us are subject to massive doses of stimuli from the outside, much of it negative. I find it is really good for me to locate places offering tranquility, peace, calmness and a sense of wellbeing. Classical music does that for me. What in your life offers you a sense of quiet serenity? Visit that space often.

Loving God Who helps each of us find serene stillness,
Help me construct barriers to the negative input I face daily.
Teach me that calmness makes me more aware of Your love.
The cacophony of the world's Babel confuses my spirit.
The culture shouts at me; let me listen for Your whispers.

SATURDAY NIGHT MOVIES

Our movie committee selects and shows a film every Saturday night in our Auditorium. Those in charge are always searching for movies they hope will please a large group of residents and attract a good crowd. The range of films presented is varied; old and new, dramas and comedies, suspense and historical, musicals and documentaries, all show up on the schedule from time to time. Some residents are sure to attend each week no matter what is offered. Others, like me, only show up occasionally for something I've heard is especially gripping or well-acted. If you tell me that Meryl Streep is the lead actress, it's certain I will attend. Because so many have hearing impairment, there are subtitles displayed with every film. It's distracting for some but necessary for others. The chairs seem to get uncomfortable after about one hundred minutes, so shorter films seem more popular than longer ones. It's amusing to watch people trudge into the auditorium with all manner of pillows, back supports, blankets and water bottles and settling in to watch the movie of the week.

Why do I go to these weekly performances? Am I merely whiling away some time and being entertained in the process? I think it's more than that. Good films and strong actors can stir my own imagination. I feel myself becoming part of the plot line while conjuring up how everything is going to work out in the end. Is your imagination stimulated similarly?

God Who helps us dream beyond our own existence,
Please show me how to use my imagination in creative ways.
Teach me to use my resourceful intellect to inspire new ideas.
Expanding my own horizons, I may open new vistas for others.

71

COLUMBUS DAY STORM

People in the Pacific Northwest still talk about the Columbus Day storm of 1962. This massive weather event was spawned by Typhoon Freda, an extra tropical cyclone in the mid-Pacific Ocean. A catastrophic combination of the jet stream, a low pressure system parked over Oregon and the remnants of the typhoon caused substantial damage particularly in the Portland area. There were wind gusts up to 116 miles per hour in the downtown area clocked on the Morrison Bridge. Other places in the metro area had gusts up to 155 miles per hour. Forty-six people died as a result of the storm. Property damage totaled about $4 billion (adjusted for inflation). Old-time residents recall the devastating power of the storm and wonder how they survived, given the conditions. Whenever the weather forecasters observe high winds, low-pressure systems and a specific jet stream, parallels are always made to that frightening day in 1962 when the historic storm hit Portland. Those who lived through it hope that it never occurs again.

Once in awhile, I encounter terrific storms in my own life. A devastating illness, the loss of a loved one, or a terrible rupture in family relationships leaves me feeling battered, alone and afraid. I must turn to my God for succor; I cannot possibly get through this by myself. Like Peter who tried to walk on the stormy sea and had to cry out, "Lord, save me!" I, too, must ask God to rescue me. How do you handle your own storms?

Loving God Who provides assistance to all who seek help,
Shelter me from my foolish pride when I face life's problems.
Let me sense Your enveloping presence when I need comfort.
Please reach out Your strong hand and pull me to safety.

THE CLIPBOARD SIGNUPS

In the foyer of our main building is a wall containing numerous clipboards. These clipboards hold notices of upcoming tours, classes, excursions, performances and shopping trips and is the place residents can sign up for participation. Some of these activities are free; others carry a cost. This is a busy place where residents check coming events for their education, entertainment and general diversion. I'm interested to see the lists of things going on and who is signing up for what. Some register for Latin, Greek, or Italian classes or a ten-week seminar on major Shakespeare plays. Who are these people? They are the ones who retain curious and active minds well into their senior years. The shopping excursions are popular with those who have given up driving an automobile and rely on community transportation to get to local markets, pharmacies and other stores. Concerts, theatrical performances and other cultural events have a devoted following of people inspired by good stage performances, dance recitals or symphonies. Help with a personal computer, lunch at a local restaurant or a foray to a gambling casino attracts enthusiastic supporters, too.

I think it is healthful to have a diversity of interests. People who regularly seek intellectual, cultural and social stimulation seem healthier, possess positive attitudes and are more interesting to be around. Do you have wide-ranging interests?

God Who provides enrichment for our minds and bodies,
I thank You for the opportunities I have to grow each day.
Help me when I feel bored or tired of my circumstances.
Too many struggle just to live while I have life in abundance.

A TRIP TO BUDAPEST

Two members of our extended family are medical doctors who were trained in Europe and immigrated to the United States in the early 1970s. Their daughter is married to our son. Joe and Marta both had distinguished careers as pathologists. Now retired, the couple spends part of their time living in Budapest, Hungary. Several years ago, they invited Evie and me to visit them in Europe. We were delighted with their gracious invitation and thoroughly enjoyed our visit. Joe and Marta were excellent tour guides and led us to many interesting places. Pest, east of the Danube, is a beautiful old city with wide, tree-lined streets, the seat of Hungary's government, a wonderful, huge central market and exotic ethnic restaurants. Buda, west of the great river, is built on hills and is full of impressive cathedrals, royal palaces and spectacular views. One lesson we learned very early: the Hungarian language is totally non-intuitive. By ourselves, Evie and I would have been completely lost facing undecipherable street signs, building names and public transport directions. Thank God Joe and Marta were there to lead us!

This vacation trip taught me a lesson. I must frequently rely on others to get something done in my own life. Just as I could not make it around Budapest on my own, I cannot make it in my daily life without the generous help of others. We like to think we're pretty self-sufficient; often, this is not the case.

God Who places others in my life to give me assistance,
Teach me to be grateful for all those I must rely upon.
They generously provide assistance when I most need it.
Remind me to be equally willing to help those who turn to me.

THE LIBRARY

In our main building is a wonderful library. Though small, its rooms are filled with outstanding reference books, videos, CDs, large-print books and selections from every genre. People move here with extensive libraries that will not fit in their living quarters. Many of these books are donated to the community library. In that way, the residents still have access to materials that are important to them without having to shelve books at home. A knowledgeable committee classifies and sorts the donations before displaying them. The rules of use are simple: take books you want and return them when you are finished. There is no checkout scheme; everything is on an honor system, which works quite well. Library usage is extraordinary. There always seem to be people browsing the stacks. In addition to the central location, books are also displayed in other spots throughout the building. Reading is a major activity for many residents. The library provides an important resource to them.

Old people like to read because they can't really participate in many other activities, right? No, that is incorrect. My neighbors are avid readers because they are committed to lifelong learning. They still have lives to lead, events to analyze, theories to investigate and history to reflect upon. The readers' mantra is, "When I read, I learn; when I learn, I am alive." Do you feel committed to learning in your later years?

God Who created all humans with a latent intellect,
Teach me how to effectively use the mental powers I have.
When I am old, encourage me to keep my faculties creative.
Lord, thank You for the gift of reading and learning.

TAMMY AND BRAD

This young couple live near our retirement community. They come on Sundays, along with their two children, to celebrate liturgy in our chapel. One weekday, they were present for daily Mass and were joined by both sets of parents. It was their tenth wedding anniversary and they asked Fr. Dick Berg to bless them on this auspicious occasion. At the end of his prayer for them, Father asked all of us in the congregation to extend our hands and join him in a final blessing of this family. What a privilege that was for all of us! Tammy briefly spoke and thanked all in the Mary's Woods community for their prayers and support. The ten years hadn't always been easy since their little girl, Ellie, is a Down syndrome child. When it was Brad's turn, he merely said he hoped all married couples would be blessed with as much joy and happiness as he and Tammy had experienced. It was an uplifting event for everyone. If life could only be so bright and full of hope every day, I thought.

I can hardly remember our tenth anniversary; those initial married years are just a blur now. Evie and I will be observing our fifty-fifth anniversary next year. I wonder what Tammy and Brad will be doing to celebrate on their milestone dates like Silver and Golden? It probably seems like the distant future to them. Little do they know about how quickly the time will pass! Are key dates like these important in your life?

God Who abundantly blesses all our vocational choices,
Help me see that I need Your grace to keep my promises.
No selected life path is always smooth; I expect challenges.
Be with me, Lord, especially during the toughest patches.

«¿DE DÓNDE ERES? SEÑOR»

You are likely to hear this question if you pass through Immigration at a port of entry in Mexico or Central America. You are being asked, "Where are you from, Sir?" For some reason, people from the United States often have difficulty answering this question, especially if the reply is attempted in Spanish. One traveler stammers, "Yo soy un Norte Americano." The patient Immigration officer replies, this time in English, "You may be a North American but so are Canadians and Mexicans. We need to narrow this down." The traveler finally recalls the answer found in the "Handy Spanish Phrase Book" purchased prior to this trip. "Yo soy un *estadounidense*." The smiling officer says, "That seems to be correct, Sir. You are a United States-er." The official waves you through Immigration while shaking his head and thinking, "Why don't these people just speak English instead of mangling our native tongue?" Many Americans are parochial about language. We believe that most people in the world speak English and, if they don't, they should. We may deserve the moniker, "The Ugly Americans."

There are hundreds of languages spoken throughout the world. When I strip away this distinction, I find most people to be much the same no matter where they're located. It's interesting how well we can establish basic communication even with those who speak an entirely different language. Have you found this to be true in your travels to other lands?

God of all people, all nations, all races and languages,
Teach me to seek similarities, not differences, with strangers.
Show me that all people strive for most of the same things.
Yes, communication may be hard; love for others should not be.

THE SANDPIPER PORCH AND PATIO

I mentioned previously that the main building on our campus was constructed as a convent. Originally built in 1906, this stately edifice also served as the training and education center for novice nuns, called postulants. The young women enrolled in this initiation program lived a rigorous and disciplined existence that offered little recreation time. When free time was available, the postulants often gathered on a covered porch at the south end of the building outside the Sandpiper Room to socialize, play their guitars and sing songs. Most of the novices were in their late teens or early twenties while perfecting their religious vocations. Now they are in their eighties or nineties living in our community as retired nuns. Of course, many changes have occurred in the intervening years. While the building has been totally refurbished, the porch still exists and an adjacent patio and pergola have been constructed.

I especially like to sit on the porch or patio during the evening hours of summer. The view of distant tall trees and the nearby apple orchard and gardens is lovely and relaxing. I sit for an extended period watching the jet contrails in the sky above, the soaring hawks and the industrious hummingbirds. What a serene experience on a warm July or August evening!

History repeats itself. What the young novices enjoyed sixty or seventy years ago, I now take pleasure in. Time stands still.

Timeless God Who always was, is and will be,
Teach me how to humanly process the passage of time.
As I age, the years seem to go by with a mere finger snap.
Slow me down, Lord; I give thanks for each new allotted day.

THE WAIT STAFF

Our two dining areas are staffed with attractive young women and men. Some are high school students in their late teens, others are in college and a few are in their mid- to late- twenties. Naturally, some are "favorites" but the entire crew is unfailingly polite, attentive and tries to satisfy every resident who comes to dine. Older folks are not always patient and can be cranky if their order takes too long, something is served at the wrong temperature or the food is not up to standard. While the manager will get involved with a serious complaint, much of the grousing is handled by the waiters or waitresses. Things usually go very smoothly and typical relations between the wait staff and the diners are pleasant and mutually respectful. The residents relate to these kids as their own grandchildren and one often hears a senior giving gentle advice to a waiter about appropriate college courses or career choices. When I asked a waitress why she liked working at Mary's Woods, she replied, "It's like having 350 grandmas or grandpas." The staff is composed of lovely young people and we feel glad to have them. Interestingly, there is a long waiting list for these jobs.

I often fail to appreciate or acknowledge others who serve my needs. Whether they are pumping gas, bagging my groceries, cutting my hair or taking my blood pressure— all servants deserve my patience, gratitude and respect. Do you agree?

God Who taught all mankind about the value of service,
Teach me to never look down on those who assist me.
Without help from others, I could not make it in this world.
Fill my heart with gratitude for those who wait upon my needs.
As you did, Lord, give me the grace to serve when I am needed.

THE ELECTORAL PROCESS

Have you ever participated in an election in the United States? No, I don't mean merely writing a check or attending an open house for your favorite candidate. I'm speaking about digging into "retail politics" with energy. That means manning a phone bank, walking precincts, stuffing envelopes, placing yard signs, writing letters to the editor, hosting a reception in your home, watching the polls on election day, writing several checks for more than you can afford to the election fund—and lots more. When I ran for City Council in Fullerton, California, my kids had the opportunity of seeing and working in the electoral process firsthand. Now adults, they still talk about the value of this experience. It was one of the most important lessons they learned during their formative years. They also learned to live with disappointment; I lost the election by eighty votes out of twelve thousand cast.

I have many acquaintances who vocally complain about our government and those who lead it. I always tell them that they cannot criticize unless they are willing to "put it all on the line" to elect someone they like better than the incumbent. I find that many are quick to grumble but are reluctant to do what it takes to change the direction of government. Unwillingness to provide major help to a candidate means that a small handful of people are able to determine the outcome of an election. Do you find that disturbing? It does not bode well for our future.

God Who said "Give to Caesar what belongs to Caesar,"
Teach me that it is a privilege to participate in government.
Solid principles will lead me to like-minded candidates.
Show me how to compete courteously and without rancor.

THE FUNERALS

Since we are a community of the elderly, funerals are a common event at Mary's Woods. Often there is a Mass for Catholics with our chaplain presiding. Families of non-Catholic faith will often invite the minister from their own church to conduct the service. Those with no church affiliation may request our Pastoral Services Director to lead a memorial service. Regardless of the circumstances, one thing always stands out; the event is mostly about the survivors, not the deceased. Loved ones, family and friends have a need to share their grief over the loss of a dear one. They also want to extol the deceased with stories about memorable incidents that defined the life of the person mourned. Telling stories into a microphone before the congregation stirs a strong emotional response. We all have empathy for someone speaking with a quivering voice and teary eyes. This cathartic experience provides healing to those who grieve. The deceased? They are already in a better, place possibly watching with bemusement.

I am usually ambivalent about funerals. My faith in the Resurrection tells me death is not the end but the beginning. And yet, my spirit is racked with grief for the human loss of a loved one, friend or neighbor. I alternately celebrate life and mourn a loss. There is always personalization; when will it be my turn? What will be said about me? Who will come? I have a detailed plan for my own funeral liturgy. How about you?

Merciful God Who loves both the living and the dead,
Let me focus on the hope of eternal life, not a human death.
Happy thoughts of a life well-led trump the pain of the loss.
Lord, show me how to live each day as if it were my last.

ASTORIA, OREGON, AND FORT CLATSOP

On the far northwest tip of Oregon stands the charming and historic city of Astoria. The city is named after John Jacob Astor who set up a fur trading post in 1811 on the site of the current city. The State of Oregon incorporated Astoria in 1876. It is often referred to as "little San Francisco" because of its many hills and quaint Victorian homes. On Coxcomb Hill stands the 125 foot tall Astoria Column where one can see beautiful ocean vistas, the mouth of the Columbia River, the Astoria-Meglar Bridge that connects Oregon and Washington, and the city center down below. About five miles west of the city is Fort Clatsop, the winter headquarters for the Lewis and Clark expedition in 1805-1806. An authentic replica of the original small fort can be explored by tourists. It is easy to see what a cold, wet, miserable existence the party experienced at this location. I think of Fort Clatsop as one of the most important historical monuments in the United States.

A casual reading about the Lewis and Clark expedition reveals men of extraordinary bravery, resourcefulness and steely resolve. Today our country faces situations even more daunting than faced by Lewis, Clark and their band of men. Where are the people we can count on today to step forward with the same courage and heroic natures needed at this time in our history? I sometimes despair about our future. Are you optimistic that we have the human resources we require?

God Who sends the saints, heroes and prophets we need,
Please give us those who will lead, inspire and galvanize us.
The world's problems seem so intractable and serious.
Lord, we need a Jefferson, a Lincoln, a John Paul II. Help us!

THE KEYBOARDISTS

We have several elderly nuns who serve as our resident keyboard players. They play the piano or organ for Catholic and ecumenical services and also help out at various social events in the community. Earlier in their careers they taught music, directed choirs and produced plays, skits and musical shows. All of them are wonderful musicians, but I'm sure they would admit to a little diminishment of their capabilities as their years added up. Each of them has forgotten more music skills than the rest of us ever had. Especially at the weekly sing-along on Monday afternoons, these ladies pound the keyboards with enthusiasm while the residents sing oldies like "My Wild Irish Rose," "I'll Be Down to Get You in a Taxi, Honey," and other favorites from the past. Although some of the nuns are well into their eighties, we never hear complaints about too much work or being over-scheduled. These nuns not only provide an important service to all the rest of us, they do so cheerfully and with a lot of pep. What wonderful ladies!

As I have gotten older, my energy level is lower, each task takes longer to complete and I am more tired at the end of the day. These nuns are great examples of people who continue to give of themselves long past the time when most people would have quit. They remind us that being old is not a good excuse for "checking out" on life. I am inspired by the model they present. It keeps me going when I might otherwise give up.

Loving God Who never gives us more than we can handle,
Bless me with strength to keep going even when it's tough.
I must learn that someone is looking to me for help or aid.
When I would like to quit, provide me courage to continue.

THOU SHALT NOT KILL

In Judeo-Christian heritage, the Ten Commandments provide a moral code of conduct for many people in today's world. One of the ten, "Thou Shalt Not Kill," presents an apparently clear- cut directive from God to abstain from taking a human life. Many believe this commandment has broader implications. For example, what about those who brutally abuse their own bodies by taking drugs, using alcohol excessively or fail to take basic precautions like using seat belts in an automobile? What do we think of people who consume so much food that they become obese? According to the National Institute of Health, two-thirds of Americans are overweight and half of them are obese. This is a growing problem that consumes massive amounts of health care resources. How do we balance Christian charity with the serious need to moderate our caloric intake? It seems harsh and judgmental to insist that obese people change their ways. If a person is obese, are they violating God's commandment, "Thou Shalt Not Kill?" This is a difficult and conflicted position. How do we resolve this?

Several years ago, my doctor told me, "Unless you lose a great deal of weight, you are certain to become a Type II diabetic." That motivated me to lose forty pounds and get my health profile back under control. That kind of weight loss is not as easy for others to achieve. I know obesity can be a death sentence for some. What is my responsibility to obese people?

Loving God Who created us as temples of the Holy Spirit,
Give me the strength and courage to care for my body.
Teach me moderation, especially with taking food and drink.
Send special blessings, Lord, to those who struggle with this.

CHECKING IN AT THE AIRPORT

Anyone who has boarded an airplane in the last ten years knows check-in and airport security is a tedious, often demeaning and, sometimes, a silly exercise. Since there are few ways to circumvent the procedures, cheerful patience is the only way to get through the process and finally board your airplane. Present your picture identification; show your ticket and boarding pass; take your shoes off; empty your pockets of change, keys and anything metal; stand quietly for a scan and pat down; open up your carry-on luggage for inspection. Each year the regulations become further intrusive. The overall goal to keep air travel safe from terrorist attack is laudable. The one-size-fits-all application of the procedures is what irritates most travelers. Why must the agents pat down infants? What is gained by obsessive screening of old grandmothers in wheelchairs? Why must they confiscate my harmless fingernail clippers? Does my metal belt buckle really pose a threat? "Grin and bear it" is the only attitude to adopt. Relax, go with the flow and you will finally arrive at the other end of the Transportation Security Agency station no worse for the wear.

I am annoyed when restrictions are placed on me. I have this arrogant idea that some rules don't apply to me. Every society needs regulations to survive without chaos. What gives me the right to believe I can operate outside the norm? Do you ever think you are exempt from rules established by society?

God Who blesses the organizations that manage society,
Teach me that all laws are established for a good purpose.
Give me patience when I discover unintended consequences.
Send graces, Lord, to all who work hard in government jobs.

COUNTING A DIFFERENT KIND OF SHEEP

When Fr. Dick Berg was suffering pain from a bad hip, he found a new way to drift off to sleep at night. Instead of counting sheep, he would randomly call up the faces of friends, neighbors or acquaintances in the sure knowledge that God loved these people unconditionally. Fr. Dick would then send his love to those same people. Instead of sheep, Father would count friends. He told us this method of getting to sleep worked for him every time. I suffer some night time pain, too, so I decided to try Father's approach. When I sought to visualize the faces of friends, the only thing I got was vivid images of people I didn't like or who had some dispute with me. Instead of putting me to sleep, I found myself agitated and restless. I tried this for several nights in a row with negative results and told Father Dick that it wasn't working for me. After looking me in the eye for several seconds, Father smiled and said, "My technique for falling asleep may not be effective for you, but in other ways it seems to be working just perfectly." In a not-so-subtle way, Father Dick was telling me that God did love my enemies; perhaps I should do the same.

I don't like to be trapped like this. I am willing to love my friends and those who are nice to me. It's uncomfortable to be reminded I am called to love my enemies, too. I keep looking for an excuse, a loophole or some way out of this requirement. I can't find one. Do you know of a way to avoid this?

God Who loves all, even those who crucified Him,
I will require special graces to love those whom I do not like.
You gave me an awesome example of loving your enemies.
But I am weak; You must give me help to do as You did.

MEN'S FAITH BREAKFAST

Twice a month a group of about fifteen men meet early to study the Bible, share ideas about religion and pray together. Those attending are diverse in age, faith background, knowledge about religious beliefs and the Bible. Within the group you will find several "flavors" of Protestants, a handful of Catholics, some who are non-affiliated and others who are just sincere seekers. These men seem to share one trait: they all are respectful of other viewpoints, even those at odds with their own beliefs. Not all sessions are inspiring but you can sense the Holy Spirit at work in every gathering. In a truly Christian way, all the men love and honor the others at the meetings. Prayers offered are heartfelt; one man may help another understand a Bible passage; the simple stories of life experiences are sincere and touching. These meetings may be an important part of the salvation story for many of the men who attend. Most men leave these meetings feeling happy that they participated. Grace has been available to all who came.

I was blessed to receive sixteen years of religious education. Participation in my parishes for fifty years provided additional training in biblical studies, catechesis and apologetics. I find it uncomfortably easy to become smug about my knowledge of all things religious. It is very humbling to encounter a simple man touched by the Spirit and in love with his Savior. His sincere faith usually trumps my knowledge and training.

God Who loves all who seek You with a sincere heart,
Show me that knowledge of You is not sufficient for piety.
Help me to see Your grace poured out to all those with faith.
Lord, give me the openness to learn about You from others.

THE MOUNTAINS

There are many vistas in the Portland area where you can get a clear view of Mt. Hood or Mt. St. Helens. No urban center in the United States is so defined by mountain peaks as the Portland-Vancouver metro area. Mt. Hood is fifty miles east of Portland. Its height is approximately 11,240 feet and is covered with twelve glaciers. In native Indian lore, the place is called "Wy'east." The mountain is valued as a skiing, snowboarding and hiking destination. It is also a dangerous place; over 150 people have died on the slopes in the past twenty years. Mt. St. Helens is fifty miles northeast of Portland. It was a beautiful conical shaped mountain 9,677 feet high until May 18, 1980 when a catastrophic eruption blew 1,500 feet off the top while the erupting material killed fifty-seven people and flattened sixty square miles. Much of the surrounding area is still barren. Mt. St. Helens continues to growl and rumble. It could provide more drama soon.

I love my frequent glimpses of the two mountains. They are so majestic when seen from a distance. Up close, they are massive, overwhelming and craggy--almost frightening in appearance. They remind me of my insignificance in the presence of an almighty and all-powerful God. I lay prostrate in the gaze of a Creator who made these mountains, but also loves me and "carved my name on the palm of His hand before I was born." My God is an awesome God.

Almighty God, I tremble in the sight of Your creation,
Mountains, oceans, rivers and forests are Your handiwork.
With my finite capacity, how am I to relate to Your greatness?
Lord, teach me that I, too, am part of Your awesome creativity.

"W. W. J. D?"

Do you remember when young people wore leather and bead bracelets and pendants displaying the letters, "W. W. J. D?" It was quite a fad for awhile. The letters stood for, *"What Would Jesus Do?"* The amulets were intended to be portable morality gauges. With His totally human-totally divine personhood, Jesus could always be expected to make the right decision in any circumstance. People faced with tough choices about relationships, sexuality, honesty, finances or types of companions, found needed perspective by considering how Jesus might have chosen in the same situation. Using that filter was not foolproof; humans with clouded intellects can still make unwise choices. Trying to base their decisions on Jesus' standards is probably helpful to many people.

I like the idea of "W. W. J. D?" My problem is I'm not sure I know what Jesus would do in every circumstance. It is not always clear—at least, to me—how Jesus would choose to act in all possible situations. For example, how would Jesus deal with an undocumented alien who committed a felony? What about a professed and devout Catholic politician who actively promoted abortion or assisted suicide? How would He treat Catholic bishops who intentionally covered up pedophile priests? What of poor people who abuse food stamps or welfare? Do you have any doubts about "W. W. J. D?"

Loving God Who blessed each of us with Free Will,
Give me the grace to choose wisely from life's options.
I can deal with the choices that seem to be straightforward.
I feel pulled in opposite directions when my options are gray.
Free Will is a mixed blessing; help me to make good decisions.

THE ANNUAL ART SHOW

Each year our community has an art show exhibiting the creative talents of our residents. The event is open to the public and draws large and enthusiastic crowds. You might think that the displayed art would be rather simple or basic. You would be wrong. The type of art showcased is diverse while the quality and creativity of the work is the output of superior artisans. You will discover stained glass, water colors, oil paintings, art created from fabric, charcoal drawings, elaborate lace, crocheting, quilting, sculpture, bookmaking and carved wood. The displays are not just "nice;" they are breathtaking. You might expect a handful of people to present their work; it is closer to fifty artists. Our community has been blessed with many talented people who willingly use their God- given skills to provide much pleasure to others.

My lack of talent in the areas noted above is legend. I deeply appreciate the skills of others even though mine are nil. God has provided each person with gifts. While I may be able to do some things well, please don't ask me to paint, sculpt or carve. The key is that we use our unique gifts to enhance our community or the lives of others. If so, we will be judged as good stewards and be rewarded for our cooperation with the blessings God has given us. What are your special gifts?

Generous God Who blesses each person with unique gifts,
Show me how to use mine for the benefit of my neighbor.
All talent is different: healing, teaching, leading, creating,
peacemaking, managing, inspiring, and being a good follower.
Teach me to celebrate the gifts of others and never to envy.
Lord, help me to get the most from what You have given me.

SUNDAY NIGHT DINNER

For the past thirty years, Evie and I have made a habit of going out to dinner on Sunday evening. When we lived in our own home, this was a nice break from cooking for ourselves. Now that we take most meals in our community dining rooms, this tradition introduces variety in our meal choices. Having lived in the same general area for over twenty years, we have developed a list of favorite nearby restaurants. We rotate through a directory that includes Chinese, Mexican, Italian, Thai, Texas Barbecue, Fish, Steak, Sushi, Soup and Salad plus everything in between. It's fun to try out a new place once in awhile. That location may, or may not, be added to our select list. We even have done an amateur restaurant guide that we share with new residents after they move in. We enjoy these Sunday outings and have become quite friendly with the proprietors of the places we frequent. We find it enjoyable to pick out our restaurant for next Sunday's dining adventure.

Most of us honor traditions. Some relate to holidays, birthdays, anniversaries or other family celebrations. Certain food is always included in the Thanksgiving dinner. A special flag is flown on national holidays. Heirloom decorations are placed on the tree at Christmas. The same vacation spot is revisited each summer. Traditions are important; they help us recall the past while we teach the young about the future. What traditions do you and your loved ones celebrate?

Loving God Who wants all of us to be happy in our lives,
Show me how tradition links my past and my future.
Let me understand how ritual customs hold families together.
Bless these practices, Lord, that give Your people happiness.

YOUTH SPORTS

Each of my fourteen grandchildren is involved in youth sports. I'm sure running around on a baseball, football, soccer or softball field or a gymnasium is far superior to being parked in front of a television set or a video game console. Like any group of youngsters, some of my grandkids are good athletes, most are average and a few try hard but don't have a lot of skill. On the positive side, one boy was on a baseball team that went to a senior Little League World Series. A girl has won state gymnastic competitions in California. A second girl was on a cheerleading team that performed at a big football bowl game in San Diego. Another boy played in a baseball tournament in Cooperstown, the home of the Baseball Hall of Fame. All the others have plenty of trophies for their participation. That's good enough for me. There is much to be said for youth sports. They teach youngsters about teamwork, competition, dealing with both success and failure, discipline, and the need for hard work. These lessons, learned at a young age, can carry over into adult life and have a positive effect.

I do have one problem: kids' activities are too tightly scheduled and overly organized. In my youth, we played pick-up games in a local park. There were no uniforms, coaches or high tech equipment—we just played. Kids don't really have much opportunity for that kind of activity now. I think it's sad.

Dear God Who especially loves and watches over children,
Please protect all kids from injury as they play their games.
Teach them to compete fairly and deal with inevitable defeat.
Let them also know the joy of winning and celebrating victory.
Lord, help them learn these lessons well as they mature.

THE WINE SOCIAL

On Monday evenings before dinner, our community has a wine and cheese social that includes a sing-along. There are a significant number of residents who come to enjoy a glass, or two, of wine, cheese cubes and pretzel sticks. Part of the group assembles around the nearby piano. "Golden Oldies" are belted out with gusto. Pitch and rhythm may be lacking but, hey, who cares? With a glass of wine and a dog-eared songbook in hand, anyone can have an enjoyable time at this weekly event. Over at the bar, two people are furiously filling glasses with red or white wine or apple cider. Since everything served at the social is free, most residents are more tolerant about the quality of the beverages being offered. People organize themselves in small groups to discuss the day's events or the latest gossip. Above the dull roar of the singing and the chattering conversations, you will frequently hear a loud chuckle, the result of an amusing story recounted. The weekly wine social is a positive activity providing a light-hearted interlude for many in our community.

It's pretty easy to become isolated when you get older. Energy levels decrease and the desire to get out and interact with others wanes. Suddenly, days go by without meaningful human contact. This is not healthy. The wine social every Monday is one small way to maintain collective interaction and have a pleasant time. Do you ever feel socially isolated?

Loving God Who created all humankind as social beings,
Help me to participate in common activity with my neighbors.
Show me how my social interaction is healthy for me.
Lord, teach us we are in this together and need each other.

MARGARET'S BENCH

Bob has been a resident for several years. He joins with others in the summer for a round of golf on Wednesday afternoons. Bob exhibits an upbeat, cheerful personality. His life revolves around family, Stanford University sporting events, frequent rounds of golf and his little kitty. A hearing impairment limits his social interaction but he is unfailingly friendly when dealing with other residents. Bob lost his wife, Margaret, several years ago. He doesn't speak about her often but, when he does, his comments are positive and loving. He had been searching for a way to honor her memory. He was shown a small garden on a corner of our campus. It was suggested that he could acquire a bench to install there. The bench would have a plaque dedicated to Margaret's memory. This was a perfect solution; Bob arranged for this to happen. Recently, a small group gathered for the dedication. The day was perfect; the prayers and the chaplain's blessings were appropriate. Bob was beaming when the little ceremony concluded. Margaret's memory had been lovingly honored.

Honoring those I love is a good thing. It may even be better if I do it while they are still living. I should remember to bring home flowers once in awhile or a small box of chocolates. It's also great to honor those who have passed on, as Bob has done. But don't wait; doing this earlier is better than later.

God Who said, "This is My beloved Son; hear Him.",
Remind me how important it is to honor my loved ones.
The tribute I pay to them is a sign of my deep respect and love.
Teach me how to reveal my admiration in meaningful ways.
Lord, show me ways to respect them in both life and in death.

GOLF OUTINGS

During the lovely summer and fall months, a group of enthusiastic residents plays a weekly round of golf at the local municipal course. Whatever skills most people had have eroded with age, although you can still spot the natural swings off the tee or the deft touch with a putter. Every player hopes today will bring the return of an easy, fluid swing, solid ball striking and accurate short play. But none of us hit the ball very far any more. Shots down the middle are rare, skulled chip shots are routine and three-putt greens are not unusual. Golf is a tough game even for skilled, younger players. For seniors like us, it can be downright cruel. Except for the occasional muttered expletive, everyone finishes the round looking forward to next week's match. It really isn't the game or score that matters; it's about being with your friends on a sunny day. Therein lies the pleasure. The quest for perfection is left in the parking lot. This is about time with companions.

Golf can be a perfect metaphor for my own life. I wish I could always have a good disposition, never utter a harsh word to a friend and always perfectly follow God's plan for me. Human nature takes over too often; I find myself performing below my expectations. "Will God continue to love me?" I wonder. Like golf, perfection in life is not attainable. God is looking for our sustained effort, that's all. Even the great saints had their human faults. Don't you agree we need to lighten up a little?

Merciful God Who understands our failures,
Teach me how to forgive myself when I make a mistake.
I would like to do everything right but weakness often prevails.
Lord, please love me even while human perfection eludes me.

THE OREGON COAST

You would think that the western continental coastline of the United States from the bottom of California to the northern tip of Washington would look pretty much the same. That is not the case. Oregon has a rugged, almost wild coast that seems uniquely different from the states north and south. 363 miles long, Oregon's coast features twelve lighthouses, eighty state parks and hundreds of jagged rocks jutting out of the ocean near the coast. U. S. Highway 101 hugs the ocean from Astoria to Brookings. There are many scenic outlooks along the highway that provide breathtaking views. Cannon Beach in the north is especially beautiful. Four miles long this deep, sandy beach is an Oregon jewel. If it could be picked up and relocated to Southern California, Cannon Beach would probably attract two million visitors per day. As it is, one can walk the entire beach and only encounter a handful of people. Native Oregonians all have their favorite locations: Seaside, Neskowin, Lincoln City, Newport, Florence, the home of massive sand dunes, Reedsport, Brookings—and many spots in between. The Oregon coast—a wondrous place to visit.

I have been fortunate to visit many places in the world, including every continent except Antarctica. Every place on earth displays awesome examples of God's creative power. It is hard for me to understand how people can deny the existence of a Supreme Being after seeing the Grand Canyon, the island of Kauai, the Matterhorn...or the hand of a newborn baby.

Almighty God Who has created an awesome world,
Teach me how to see Your handiwork that exists everywhere.
Thank you, Lord, for filling the earth with such majesty.

THE COMMUNION SERVICE

On Monday mornings, no priest is available to celebrate Mass in our chapel. Instead, there is a Communion Service using the scripture readings of the day and including the distribution of the Holy Eucharist to those attending. One of our nuns, or a selected lay person, performs this service. Both Evie and I are privileged to occasionally lead this liturgy. There is a set order for this ritual and all the prayers to be recited are printed out for the leader. One portion of the ceremony requires the creative input from the officiant. After the scripture readings are complete, a brief homily should be presented to the congregation. This represents the leader's thoughts about how the readings might apply to our lives this day. Creating this homily can cause some anxiety. "What should I say? I don't think I'm qualified to be doing this!" We take comfort in the Gospel of Matthew 10: 19-20. "...Do not worry about how you are to speak or what you are to say. For it will not be you who speaks but the Spirit of your Father speaking through you." Thank you Lord, for that assurance.

I'm not shy but I have passed up a lot of opportunities to offer input at parish, community and business meetings. I think, "Maybe my ideas are silly; what if my arguments are ridiculed? No thanks, I'll just keep my mouth shut and not take the chance of embarrassing myself." Have you ever done that?

God Who calls upon people to lead if they are so gifted,
Help me not to waste any talents You have loaned to me.
I may be afraid but that isn't a good reason to remain silent.
If I have been gifted with leadership, show me what to do.
I will trust You, Lord, to give me the right words to say.

RESIDENT BIRTHDAY PARTIES

One day each month is set aside to celebrate every resident who has a birthday during that month. One of our dining rooms is reserved for this event and festively decorated. The menu is especially inviting; free wine and a lovely cake are part of the service, so everyone really feels like they have been to a party. Each person's day of birth is announced and applauded—the year is ignored. Usually some brief toasts are offered to all those marking another little milestone on life's journey. Each succeeding year brings some new people who just joined the community. There are also some familiar faces who no longer attend because of infirmity or, perhaps, they have passed on. The birthday party is a nice tradition and gently reminds all that we're one year older. When the event concludes, each person probably believes they will return next year to celebrate again. That may, or may not, be the case.

My birthday is really just a square on a calendar. I usually don't feel much different on the day before my birth date or on the day after. It is just another milestone like the ones I pass on the highway while in my auto. It's foolish to think that the year's count will ever get smaller. I'm ticking off more time heading toward eternal life. How do you feel about birthdays?

God Who allots a certain number of days to each person,
Teach me to mark the passage of days in an appropriate way.
None of us know the hour when our earthly life will end.
Show me how to live every moment with enthusiasm and hope.
Lord, when I finally see You face to face, wrap me in Your arms.

OREGON'S CLIMATE

No area in the country takes more grief about its weather than Portland. People have said to me, "Oh, you're from Portland. It rains there every day, right?" Someone else told me, "I've heard that the four seasons in Oregon are "getting ready to rain, raining, still raining and road construction." Yes, we have gray, dripping skies from November through May. Once in awhile we will get a little mid-winter snow or ice. But please know that there are twenty-seven major cities in the United States that get more annual rainfall than Portland. Late spring, summer and autumn usually provide us with gorgeous, warm and sunny days. Only a few days each year top 90^0 and 100^0 is rarely exceeded. Summer humidity is mild, the insect population is manageable and being north of the 45th Parallel makes for long, sultry summer evenings. In other words, the climate in Portland is generally great—maybe even better than where you live. We're America's best kept secret.

I don't want to rub it in. Portland really has desirable climate, believe it or not. But if you live in California, Nevada, New York, Utah, Minnesota—and a lot of other places—you have plenty to brag about, too. Even though we were taught in song that "Ireland was sprinkled with stardust by God," we really know that His blessings have been distributed throughout the world. So, each of us has good reason to be pleased about where we live. Don't you feel fortunate to live where you do?

God Who has uniquely blessed every location on earth,
Teach us to be grateful for the benefits of our region.
Help us to appreciate the blessings of the place we live.
Lord, show us how to be thankful for all You have given us.

11:59:59 P. M.

The next tick of the clock will announce midnight. This is the dead of the night, the blackest and most dangerous time of the day. Dawn is hours away so we must navigate through the next dreary period in darkness, feeling our way along and not knowing what may be looming ahead. It is the worst time in our twenty-four hour cycle. We dread it when midnight comes.

...Or

The next tick of the clock announces the first moment of a bright new day. It is the time we rejuvenate ourselves for the challenges that dawn will bring. The dim red glow on a distant horizon tells us that the morning sun is just a few short hours away. We rest peacefully in eager anticipation of the warming sun's arrival. Midnight is the best moment of the day.

Which of these scenarios speaks to your view of life? Does each new day bring you dread or hope? Do you worry about what is ahead or anticipate what life may have in store? Do you sense a loss of control as you age or are you willing to snuggle in the arms of God Who loves you unconditionally?

I am an ardent advocate for people developing a personal "exit strategy" for their lives. Try to figure out how you're going to deal with "what's next." Turn to God for help with this plan. Relinquish control; God has more time than you do anyway.

Loving God,
Help me to find You and "what's next" for me.
I know You are there but sometimes You feel distant.
Teach me to reach out and embrace You, ever present God.

EPILOGUE

The sub-title of this book—"*Where the Elderly Find God*"—needs some explanation. It can be said that none of us, young or old, ever *find* God; He has never been lost and is always present to us. Sometimes in our busy lives, we get so involved in earthly cares that we forget about our faithful God. So, it is more a question of *discovering* or *rediscovering* God rather than *finding* Him. I hope some passages in this book have helped you experience the Divine Presence more fully in your own life.

As we age, it's probably true that we spend more time thinking about a personal encounter with our Creator at the end of our earthly life. What will it be like to see God face to face, I wonder? How will we communicate? Am I going to experience some real surprises? All of this is in the future; I have no idea when this event will take place. I also spend some time thinking of my past relationship with God, the joys and blessings I have received, the mistakes I have made, the opportunities that were lost. This is all history, past tense. While it has formed me in some way, there is nothing I can do to change what has already occurred. It is a good thing that God is all-merciful. I need to have my flaws overlooked.

We conclude that the future is unknowable and the past is unchangeable. Our true relationship with God is always happening *now*, in the present tense. May all of us savor and hold tight to God who is always with us during the current moment of our lives. Truly, eternal life has already begun for all of us in the here and now. Amen.